THE INDIANS STEPPED OUT
OF THE WOODS

All three had their laser assault rifles nonchalantly at ready positions. They walked forward, easily confident.

When they came to a halt, some ten feet off, the eyes of both the troopers narrowed as they looked at the heavy rifles.

Buffalo Dong said easily, "Ugh. Don't try it, white men. You're covered by more than fifty warriors, including two machine gun teams. Aravaipa, get their guns."

The war chief went over to the red police vehicle, fished around in the dash compartment, and came up with a portable tape machine.

He held it to his mouth, flicked the activating stud and said into it: "The Marijuanero Apache Tribal Council herewith declares war upon the United States of the Americas and will remain in the field until victorious or until the last warrior has been slain."

HOME SWEET HOME: 2010 A.D.

Mack Reynolds with Dean Ing

A DELL/EMERALD BOOK

Published by
Dell Publishing Co., Inc.
1 Dag Hammarskjold Plaza
New York, New York 10017

Dell ® TM 681510, Dell Publishing Co., Inc.

ISBN: 0-440-03658-5

Printed in the United States of America

First printing—September 1984

In America the monogamous nuclear family—the bread-winner father, housewife mother, and children—is not only the current ideal—our entire system of laws, customs, attitudes, and human service delivery systems are set up to support the monogamous nuclear family, as though all Americans lived in such a family. But most Americans do not. The 1970 U.S. Census revealed that only 37% of the American population lived in a nuclear family, and fewer still in a monogamous nuclear family. Most of us lived in single households, or dual-working-parent families, or single-parent families, or childless couples, or post-childrearing couples, or extended families or in some other type of household. Since over half of the married population has been involved in adultery or some other form of extramarital sex, the number of people in monogamous nuclear families amounted to less than 19% of the population.

James W. Ramey
The Futurist, August 1975

Chapter One

It was four o'clock in the afternoon, give or take a half hour, when Sweet Alice entered the saloon of the Chutzpa family. Originally, when the family built their connected underground houses, they'd called this area the living room, or the recreation room. But at the time, Colleen had a culture complex and insisted they call it the salon. The French pronunciation rapidly shifted to reflect the large quantities of excellent homemade hooch consumed there; 'saloon' it was.

This is what the saloon looked like:

It was the biggest room in the biggest of the three buildings and faced onto the patio, complete with windows so that you could see the flowers and trees and the fountain in the middle that usually didn't fount. Sometimes Ron would putter around with it, but Ron wasn't much of a plumber. When they had built the house, the Professor was hot to have a pool with carp in it. According to

Huxley's *After Many a Summer Dies the Swan*, a carp can
live practically forever and the Professor wanted to see.
But a carp in the Chutzpa family pool would have had to
carry a good luck charm and its own water canteen. Opposite the patio, the wall of the saloon was practically all
one-way glass. From the outside the glass looked like new
grass and you had to get fairly close before you could see
that it wasn't just more of the greenery that extended up
the hill. The windows looked out on a stretch of prairie,
miles of rolling hills and then the Sangre de Cristo mountains in the far background. It was a view most city-
dwellers would have killed for.

In spite of her culture complex, which seemed to come
and go, Colleen hadn't prevailed when it came to furnish-
ing the saloon. Every kind of furniture jostled its distant
cousin, some of it homemade (especially pieces favored
by Ron, whose spirit had once or twice moved him to
carpentry). A moderate sized bar occupied one end of the
saloon and a life-size Tri-Di screen was built into the wall
of the other end. Scattered around were a few tables and a
desk, two couches and odds and ends of chairs and stools.
The stools were handmade of mesquite, a leftover of the
handicrafts stage the family had since largely outlived.

There were no rugs, hand-crafted or otherwise. The
Professor had read somewhere that the early Sumerians of
Ur had made their floors of adobe mud and then treated
them with ox blood and milk, repeating the treatment
perhaps once a month and polishing like bejazus. When
excavated some six thousand years later by modern
archeologists, these floors were still in perfect shape, looked
like linoleum with a lustrous rich, bronze-like finish. The
family was giving it a try in the saloon. Brick floors, first
treated with *chapote* and then waxed, and sometimes rug-

strewn, could be found throughout the rest of the rooms in all three buildings, but the floor of the saloon was enduring the Mesopotamian treatment. Despite a faint scent that was half-gory, half-curdled, it was a damned comfortable room.

Sweet Alice came in, her khaki shorts soiled and rumpled, her hair every which way, and looking banged up in general. She found Rusty sitting off to one side running one of the old-time movies from their video disc collection. For Rusty and the Doc, who were old enough to remember the movies, these epics had the power to infect with a two-hour case of nostalgia. The rest of the family had a tendency to groan when Rusty brought out her treasured *Gone With the Wind* again, or when Doc insisted on an evening with Mr. Laurel and Mr. Hardy. Now she was watching Errol Flynn kill off Japs by the score in the Philippines. He carried a submachine gun that was a direct descendent of the six-shooter of the Old Cinematic West. That is, the Tommy gun carried a 20-round clip, but Errol was able to shoot it three hundred times without reloading.

The only other member of the family present was the Professor, slumped off in another corner of the huge L-shaped room, reading an old fashioned honest-to-Gutenberg book. Where he got them, nobody seemed to know.

The Professor looked like this: He wore the look of a man with a permanent toothache and, at the age of forty or so, had already given up pulling his stomach in. He defiantly wore old-fashioned glasses, in this day of contact lenses and optical surgery, and pince-nez glasses at that. His washed-out slightly green eyes looked tired within moments after a good night's sleep and, had his beard not been permanently removed some years before, he probably would have gone without shaving three or four days in a row. He didn't give a damn about his looks and inwardly prided himself on the fact. He was thin, save for the pot belly, and the lousiest lay in the family. He looked like a middle-aged Jimmy Stewart playing the part of a disgruntled, disillusioned failure who wondered why in the hell the Fates had dealt him no face cards.

They both loooked up when Sweet Alice came through the door from the patio.

Rusty blurted, "Christ! What happened to you?"

Sweet Alice was obviously exhausted. In fact, she could hardly walk. She ran the back of her dirty left hand over her lips and said, "You know that Dobreganas boy, the one I mentioned was always following me?"

"Yes, of course," the Professor said. He had come to his feet, his eyes a bit wider than was his wont, since the Professor played life chill.

Sweet Alice slumped down into a chair, still breathing deeply.

"He raped me."

Sweet Alice looked like this: She was lush, without any suggestion of being fat. She had the figure that would have won contests thirty years before, when such institutions were in vogue. By current standards, her mammary glands were a bit too large, though they were going to be awfully interesting for, say, another ten years. Her waist was teeny small, but would it remain so? Her buttocks were a Greek dream, even on a girl. In short, Sweet Alice's body was a very edible looking dish indeed, and should have been served with a spoon. Alas, as so often, her face was empty; all but vacuous. Oh, fine blond hair, in the Swedish-Finnish tradition, impossibly blue of eye, always smiling of generous mouth but, to be brutally frank, one got the impression of a lamp unlit. She looked like Goldie Hawn playing a dizzy blond.

"Good grief," the Professor said. "Should I call Doc?" He and Rusty both bustled over to her.

"No. But how about a drink?" Sweet Alice said. She looked as though she could use one.

The Professor hurried over to the bar, picked up a bottle of fierce applejack and poured her a noble slug. He ignored the carafe of water and didn't bother to get ice from the built-in refrigerator. He hurried back with the potion.

Rusty had sat herself on the arm of the chair Sweet Alice was in and said, "What happened, dear? Perhaps we should phone the police in Coronado." She put her arm about the younger woman anxiously, comfortingly.

Alice took the drink and tossed it back, breathed deeply again, and put the glass down on the coffee table next to her. It was the table with one short leg that Zack had made when they were all doing furniture and which had originally been meant to be of ordinary height but had been wonky-legged on completion. Zack had solved the problem by cutting down the other three legs but when he was through, he had cut one of them off too much and started all over again. It was now about the height of one of those Japanese deals, a few inches off the floor, and one leg was still short. They had finally stuck a wedge of cardboard under the culprit. Colleen had demanded one night to put to a vote whether or not to throw it out, but it had a nice top and the majority voted her down, the Twins being especially vociferous, since the table was short enough that they could climb up on it.

Sweet Alice said, "It was that overgrown cube, Jesus Dobreganas."

"Jesus?" Rusty said.

"That's pronounced *Hey-Zeus*, in Spanish," the Professor told her, standing in front of them and squinting down, upset. "The Spanish are like the Moslems. They aren't taking any chances of failing to ingratiate themselves with the powers that be. Practically all Moslem men are named Mohammed, and the women Fatima, and almost as many Spanish men are named Jesus or Angel. That's pronounced *Ahn-heel*. And possibly half of their women are named Mary."

"All right, all right, give us the language lecture later," Rusty said to him, and turned back to Sweet Alice. "What did he do, dear? Are you hurt?"

Rusty looked like this: At forty-odd she was one of those plain women, none of whose features are particularly bad but whose faces just don't add up to handsomeness. The freckles didn't help. While most lose their freckles about age twelve or so, Rusty didn't. In fact, if anything, she went on to acquire more. Her washed out, gray-streaked hair was too thin and she insisted on wearing it in a pony tail, which looked bedraggled on her no matter how recently she had combed it. She was also practically concave in the breast department, much too long of waist, boyish of hips, and a little bowed of stocky legs. She looked like a cowgirl of the Old West, or possibly a short Amazon right out of mythology. In brief, she was the wiriest, drabbest female of the family and nobody had ever figured out why she was popular with men.

"No, I'm not hurt," Sweet Alice said. "Just fagged. I was walking along that path toward the ruins of the old pueblo, looking to see if the berries were ready for picking. And after awhile I got the feeling I was being watched. You know. And finally I spotted him. Jesus. I mean Jesus Dobreganas, not the one on the cross. And when he saw I saw him he came running. And he grabbed me and started rassling me around. And I tried to argue with him. It was all gravel and sand and cactus and everything. But he dragged me over to the shade of one of the old adobes.''

"Oh, you poor kid," Rusty said. "Couldn't you get away?"

"Well, no. Not exactly. And he pushed me down and he pulled my shorts off. Real rough."

"Bastards," the Professor said meaninglessly, but probably referring in general to the young machos of Coronado, who lived by the mores of the past.

"Then what?" Rusty said, in a soothing albeit anxious voice.

Alice put her hands up in a gesture of the obvious and she shrugged. "Then he raped me."

Rusty closed her eyes in pain. "What'd you do, Alice, when he finished?"

Sweet Alice said, her blue eyes indignant and as though nothing was more obvious, "I raped him back."

Rusty and the Professor looked at her blankly, as though they'd gone to the john and, only afterwards, found there was no paper.

Sweet Alice said with righteous satisfaction, "When I left him, he was limp as a shrimp. Kind of pale. And it's a long walk back to town."

Chapter Two

Bitter Joe was at loose ends. The night before, he had inadvertently suckered himself into going through a work in the National Data Library Banks on Japanese art, a subject in which he was little interested. Just about when he was going to fade it off the screen, he came across a reference to the favorite sexual position of the Nipponese. For reasons unknown, it made him wonder what the favorite position of, say, the Romans might have been, so he dialed Sex on his Library Booster Screen, narrowed it down and finally got what he wanted, complete with illustrations taken from the murals in the whore house—they called it the Lupanar—in Pompeii. Still not really interested, he idly dialed for the same material on how the Macedonians did it. Before he was through, and at dawn's early light, Bitter Joe had become an authority on the sexual positions of the ancients, a subject in which he had no real concern whatsoever. Unfortunately, he was cursed with an eidetic memory and undoubtedly would retain until death such items as the fact that Phoenecian prostitutes were the first women ever to wear lipstick, painting their mouths red to indicate that they practiced fellatio.

So in mid-afternoon, after sleeping fitfully through the day, he felt as drowsy as he appeared.

Bitter Joe looked like this: It didn't make much difference what you said, the twist of his mouth indicated that he doubted you. Though by no means to the manor born, he had an expression once de rigueur among the British aristocracy when looking upon one of the lower classes, nostrils slightly high. In an age when medical science could provide you with as much hair as you wished, wherever you wished and any color you wished, Bitter Joe's hairline receded to a point exactly halfway to the back of his head. He couldn't care less. He looked like Fredric March at the age of 55, playing Clarence Darrow defending a black before a white Alabama jury, on a molesting-a-white-child charge.

With nothing he could think of that he particularly wanted to do, he headed over for the Kid's Kolony. The theory was that all adults, senior adults in particular, were to make themselves periodically available as tutors to the family's four children (six if you counted JoJo and Sweet Alice). The definition of tutoring was up for grabs. What it amounted to was that you became the target for any questions they wanted to shoot at you and you did your best— which was apt to be insufficient, particularly when the Wizard was on the firing line.

The Kid's Kolony was only a hundred meters from the main family house and was about half its size, though it had originally been built with more youngsters in mind. They just hadn't materialized, as yet at least. The top and sides of the Kolony were covered with trees, bushes, wild flowers and grass and looked like part of a gentle wood, as did the rest of the family estate. You got quite close before you saw that there was a dwelling below the mound.

As Bitter Joe approached, one of the many cottontails broke cover and made an excited dash for it, though by this time any rabbit with half a brain would've been so used to the Family it would've lined up for chow call three times a day.

Bitter Joe came to the naturally camouflaged short stairway that led down to the patio and the rooms surrounding it, and made his way to the alleged schoolroom, the largest chamber in the dwelling. Its other rooms consisted of a playroom, a nursery and various bedrooms for those old enough to wish a sanctum of their own. In actuality, only the Wizard and Sweet Alice lived in the Kid's Kolony bedrooms and on Sweet Alice's part it was sheer laziness. She had simply never made the effort to move over to the adult quarters of the family complex. The Twins and Ruthie were in the Nursery, to Ruthie's disgust. Ordinarily, the family adults took turns sleeping in the Kid's Kolony, in a room adjoining the Nursery.

The family had its own ideas about the schooling of its youth, and of the continuing education of its adults for that matter. They had decided that at least four-fifths of what was usually taught did not apply to what the child needed in future life; and that what kids did need to know, such as sex education and how to make money, was either taboo or ignored.

Bitter Joe was old enough to remember a news release from the U.S. Office of Education in 1975 which revealed the results of a four-year study. Apparently more than 23 million adult Americans were functionally illiterate, meaning that they were incapable of reading help-wanted ads, making change, shopping for food intelligently, locating health and community services, or understanding basic tax and insurance concepts. Twenty percent of citizens 16 to 65 "functioned only with difficulty" in the everyday adult world and another 34 percent "were functional but not proficient" said the report. Almost 35 million persons flunked such tests as reading a grocery ad or problems of simple arithmetic. Twenty percent of those surveyed didn't know the meaning of the notice, "We Are Equal Opportunity Employers." And 14% could not properly write a bank check, not to speak of the fact that 27% were unaware that normal body temperature was 98.6 degrees F. The word 'celsius' was not in their lexicons.

The Chutzpa family, along with a good many others in the country, had decided the hell with Latin, Geometry and such unless the kid's interests ran to lines where such studies were called for. Utilizing the Auto-Teachers, connected with the National Data Banks, and the Library Banks, the family let them more or less educate themselves. They saw that the youngsters got their basic reading, writing and arithmetic, but from there on in let them go to hell in their own way. They had found that kids, in general, wanted to learn how to read and write and do basic mathematics; they needed it to conduct even a kid's way of life. From there on in, it was up to the individual. Whether he would study, and what he would study, was up to him. In the family, at least, it had led to as wide a divergence as Sweet Alice and the Wizard who, at the age of fifteen, was currently involved in reading the Encyclopedia Britannica and had thus far gotten to the letter "J". Sweet Alice could add and subtract but had her difficulties with long division and preferred to get her news, to the extent she wanted it at all, from the Tri-Di broadcasts rather than a newspaper.

Bitter Joe found that the classroom was getting a better play than usual, all four of the younger children being present. Ordinarily, one of the adults would have been sitting around to supervise, give suggestions, answer questions, or whatever, but evidently today the spirit hadn't moved any of them to fulfill that duty. Nine-year-old Ruthie was at one of the six desks, supplied gratis by the Department of Education, and peering into an Auto-Teacher screen. Her usually sensuous mouth, if that term is applicable to a nine-year-old, and in this case it was, looked somewhat slack. The Wizard was to one side of the room, watching a newscast on the Tri-Di. The four-year-old Twins were demolishing with great elan a set of educational toys that had also been provided, unsolicited, by the Department of Education. Local Education Department officials in the nearest town, Coronado, were inclined to wince when it came to the Chutzpa children but since they invariably passed the yearly examinations with flying colors, indeed with jet-propelled colors, there was nothing for it. Theoretically the Professor had them in charge and the Professor had a degree in education, after all.

The kids didn't bother to look up when Bitter Joe entered. He wandered over toward Ruthie and stood momentarily next to her desk.

He said, "Hi, Ruthie. What spins?"

She said, without looking up, "Ummm."

Bitter Joe tried to smile benignly but wasn't equipped for it. He said, "Any questions accumulated?"

Ruthie said, still without tearing her eyes from the screen, "What does French mean, Uncle Joe?"

Ruthie looked like this: At the tender age of nine, she

was—there was no other word for it—sexy. Average weight, average height for her age, somehow she managed to project a *wanton* quality, in a childish sort of way. Had somebody supplied her with a falsies, cosmetics and adult clothing, she could have passed for a fully mature midget. She was sloe of brown eyes, red of hair which she wore to her shoulders in a sultry hairdo, and her still childish hips managed to sway in walk. The average male was inclined to think, upon viewing her for the first time, *that's going to be one hot dish in another five years* and then revise the time estimate downwards. And women were inclined to think, inwardly, *good God, is the competition getting that young?* She looked like a nine-year-old edition of Brigitte Bardot.

Bitter Joe said, "Why, the French are the people who live over in France, in Common Europe, honey. The capital of their country is Paris and . . ."

"No, no," Ruthie shook her head definitely. "This says she wanted to French him."

Bitter Joe said bitterly, "What are you reading? No, don't tell me, on second thought."

But Ruthie said, "It's *My Secret Life*, by Anonymous. He sure writes a lot of books. It's got an introduction by G. Legman. What's quim?"

Bitter Joe closed his eyes in pain. "Never mind," he muttered. "You'll undoubtedly figure it out before the chapter's through."

He shook his head and went over to the Wizard. He sank into a chair next to the fifteen-year-old, but didn't look at the news commentator who was holding forth. Bitter Joe had a theory that following the news was responsible for half the ulcers in the world.

However, in the role he had assumed, he had to say something. "Hi, Wizard. What spins?"

The teenager didn't take his eyes from the projection. He said, "Evidently, the heads of the Dixiecrats."

"Who the hell are the Dixiecrats?"

"One of the minority parties at the Second Constitutional Convention. The State Religion question has been tabled. The Baptists mounted a filibuster."

"State Religion?" Bitter Joe said, in the same tone he might have used to say, "cancer?"

"The Reformed Agnostic Church is against it," the Wizard told him, explaining practically nothing.

Bitter Joe didn't want to think about some of that, such as who in the hell the Reformed Agnostics were, so he said, "What about the Dixiecrats, or whatever you called them?"

"They want the new Revised Constitution to re-establish slavery. They claim the Darkies never had it so good and, besides, that Lincoln's Emancipation Proclamation was unconstitutional."

Bitter Joe looked at him blankly and couldn't think of anything to say except, "Well, was it?"

"Yes."

Bitter Joe had no inclination to get into an argument with the Wizard. Nobody in the family wanted to get into an argument with the Wizard. He said, "What else is new?" feeling a gnawing in his stomach. Now he knew damn well ulcers were caused by assimilating the news—especially those sudden bulletins which a few media mavens such as "Annabelle" could inject into the Tri-Di on short notice.

The Wizard said, "The Marijuanero Apaches have gone on the warpath."

Bitter Joe eyed him.

The Wizard looked like this: He had shot up the past year or so to the point where he probably had his full height at the age of fifteen but in doing so had become overly thin and had the gawkiness of the teenager. Fine hair had begun to manifest itself on his face but he had refused to have it permanently depilated since he wanted to raise a mustache, that leftover, along with beards, of yesteryear. He was irritable and nervous and, like the Professor, insisted upon wearing anachronistic glasses; in his case, large, black-rimmed ones. He knew damned well he was smarter than anyone he'd ever come in contact with and his attitude admitted, nay proclaimed, the fact. He was one twitchy, objectionable snot and the best that was thought of him in the family was that he might grow out of it. But it seemed unlikely. He looked like a stereotype Quiz Kid of the 1930s.

Bitter Joe said, "Who in the hell are the Marijuanero Apaches and what'd'ya mean they're on the warpath?"

The Wizard said condescendingly, "Don't you ever watch Tri-Di?"

"No," Bitter Joe told him. "I used to when I was your age, until my damn' eyes nearly fell out. It was TV in those days. Only two dimensional."

"Why did you stop?"

"They finally discontinued the commercials. They were the funniest part."

"Well, the Marijuaneros are the smallest surviving Apache tribe. They have, or had, most of Geronimo County north of here as their reservation. It was evidently the crummiest Indian reservation in the country."

"That rates a Nobel Prize for crumminess," Bitter Joe said. "What happened?"

The Wizard was never adverse to displaying his knowledge. He said, "They were the wisenheimers of the Apaches. Back in the old days they used to supply most of the medicine men with their alkaloids. At any rate, they scraped enough together to send one tribe member back to Harvard Business School and he got through with honors. Then he came back just when the Indian Revival fad hit the country. Do you remember that?"

"Yes," Bitter Joe said. "Hell, I can remember back to the hula hoops and even the Davy Crockett fad. I had a coonskin cap and . . ."

The Wizard overrode him. "So he talked the council of chiefs into sending him to Japan and there, on credit, he ordered a whole selection of bows and arrows, feathered headdresses, tomahawks, peace pipes, moccasins—the whole shebang. And the tribe went into business."

"The fad only lasted two or three years, but that was enough. They coined money and with it they sent all of their young people to college, everything from MIT to Texas A and M."

Bitter Joe said, "When I was your age we had a spate of Texas Aggie jokes. Did you hear about the Aggie that . . ."

The Wizard overrode him again. "I'm giving you background," he said condescendingly, to the point where Bitter Joe contemplated awarding him the back of his hand in return. "That's when some government surveyers discovered uranium on the reservation."

"I can see it coming," his elder said. "Like when gold was discovered in the Black Hills in Sioux country. Like when oil was discovered in Oklahoma in Cherokee country. Like when the white settlers found that the Nez Perce reservation had some of the most fertile farm land in Idaho. Like when . . .''

The Wizard sighed at the interruption. "So they've gone on the war path, under their war chief, Buffalo Dong.''

Bitter Joe's face reflected disbelief. "That can't be his name.''

The teenager said patiently, "His real name is some-thing Indian, but when he was with the Green Berets in the Asian War the others couldn't pronounce it so they called him Buffalo Dong, for some reason or other. He evidently got the nickname after a leave in Japan with several of his buddies.''

Bitter Joe refused to consider the ramifications of that biographical datum.

The Wizard went on. "At any rate, he won the Congressional Medal of Honor, because he was an expert at demolition. Evidently, he blew up half the Mekong Delta.''

"Green Berets,'' Bitter Joe protested. "Why, that'd make him as old as I am.''

"They say he was just a boy when he enlisted.''

Bitter Joe said, with a snort, "So, we haven't done any better with our Final Solution of the Indian Problem than the Nazis did with the Jews. We're still working on it.''

"How do you mean?''

"Oh, we anticipated them by a century and a half. Rosenberg, Hitler's party theoretician, must have studied American history. The Constitution was ratified in 1788 and the United States began, thirteen small colonies on the Atlantic seaboard. We started our Final Solution to the Indian Problem immediately and less than a hundred years later, in 1886, Geronimo surrendered, winding up the so-called Indian Wars. It wasn't war, it was massacre. We butchered them from coast to coast, winding up at Wounded

Knee where the last Plains tribe who had any guts left in them were polished off with Gatling guns—men, women and children. By that time, the only Indians left were misfits, poverty-stricken drunks, beggars, and bums, who were ordered away to the most desolate areas of the country, the equivalent of concentration camps. And like I said, if gold, or oil, or anything else worth having turned up on one of their reservations, they were kicked off that too. And any supposed treaty, permanently signed, was torn up by us super-free Americans.''

The Wizard didn't like the limelight to be taken from him. He said, ''I like the numerical facts of that last so-called Indian War you mentioned. When Geronimo went on the warpath the last time, General Crook immediately fielded five thousand soldiers and five hundred mercenary Indian scouts, plus thousands of irregular civilian militia. On top of this, when Geronimo's warriors slipped across the border, they were subjected to the attacks of thousands of Mexican troops, mobilized against them. And how many men did he have in his whole war party? Twenty-four.''

Bitter Joe knew when he was upstaged. He said, ''Well, what's all this about Buffalo Dong?''

The Wizard could be condescending again, in his superior knowledge. ''Evidently, the Final Solution to the Indian Problem, as you call it, isn't final as yet. There are some new angles. Buffalo Dong and his men don't fight with bows and arrows against repeating rifles any more. He learned about such things as plastique in the army. They say that he claims they'll blow up every bridge, dam and power line in Arizona and New Mexico. On top of that, some of the Marijuaneros went back east to law school. It's rumored that the Apaches are taking their case to the Reunited Nations."

"Oh, great," Bitter Joe said, standing. "Every country in the world claims to have solved its colonial and minority problems, at long last. And now these Indians are going to sound off about American persecution. We'll be as popular in the General Assembly as a new strain of king-sized crotch cattle."

The Wizard, for once, was uninformed. He had to say, "Crotch cattle?"

"Crabs," his so-called tutor told him. "Body lice. I suppose men's-room graffiti were before your time. I recall one that used to go:

> There's no use standing on the seat,
> The crabs in here can jump six feet."

Bitter Joe went over to the Twins, leaving a baffled Wizard behind him.

The Twins had finished off the Educational Toys. Bitter Joe assumed that they'd lifted the hammer and saw they'd enthusiastically utilized from the family tool shed in The Barn.

The Twins looked like this: They were two unkempt little cherubs. On second thought, they were more like two curly blond-haired, sparkling blue-eyed, chubby-legged imps right out of Dante's stamping grounds. Offhand, nobody could ever remember seeing them with shoes on, nor in more than one grimy garment at a time, and that khaki or denim shorts, the standard garb of the family, male or female. They were the kind of child no sane adult would trust behind his back. They looked like the four-year-old Shirley Temple, though not as sweet and neat by a pair of damn sights.

Bitter Joe stood with hands on hips, looked down at the debris, and said, "Hi, Twins."

And one of them bothered to look up, hacksaw in hand, and said, "Hi, Uncle Joe."

"I see you did a complete job on that," Bitter Joe said, approvingly.

Chapter Three

The man who called himself John Shay brought his rental hovercar to a halt on one of the campus drives about a quarter of a kilometer from the unostentatious building that was his destination. The station was located on the outskirts of Princeton University City.

He got out of the car, having parked it inconspicuously in the shade of two of the trees which lined the driveway at this point, and looked up and down. Three of the high-rise buildings which comprised the University were within eyesight and he viewed them without expression. He had never been in a University City before. He inwardly shrugged and began strolling easily toward the building to which he had been summoned. As he drew nearer, he eyed it. Set back away from the drive, it looked somewhat like an old-time southern plantation mansion. He didn't know it but a double score of years earlier it had originally been used as a research center for some esoteric new weapons system

27

that had never come off, or, at least, by the time it had been perfected, events had passed it by. Like so many far-out projects researching more efficient methods of depleting the human race, it was antiquated before ever being operative.

He started up the narrower driveway which led to the small parking area in front of the station and to the white columned porch which was the main entry.

John Shay looked like this: He was in his mid-thirties, which you didn't discover until you had taken him in more carefully. At first view, he could have been judged ten years younger. He wasn't a big man, but slight of build and deceptively gentle of movement. His litheness was another quality that didn't immediately come through because he seemed to move lazily. He was blondish, washed-out blue of eye, and probably, when in his teens, had been considered the typical American boy-next-door. Aside from slightly buck teeth, he was moderately handsome. Not one in twenty would have suspected his ancestry. In actuality, his people had come from the Lake Como region, in the north, and there was probably Tyrolian blood in his veins. He looked like Alan Ladd playing one of those parts where you didn't discover he was a gangster until you were wrist-deep in your second box of popcorn.

At the entry to his destination, a conservatively dressed, pleasant-looking type smiled and said, "Sorry, sir. This area is off limits. Uh, restricted."

John Shay, expressionless, took out his wallet, flipped it open, handed it over, and said, "I'm expected."

The other looked at the credentials, closed the wallet and handed it back again. "Of course, Mr. Shay," he said.

When John Shay had passed on, the other put his mouth next to his wrist watch and harangued it.

There were six steps leading up to the porch. Shay ascended them and came to the second conservatively dressed, seemingly easygoing type, standing there. This one bore a clipboard in his hands.

He smiled a small smile and said, "Mr. Shay?"

"That's right," John Shay said. When he talked, his lips parted only slightly. He brought out his wallet again and flicked it open, but the other only glanced at it as he checked the clipboard.

"Your appointment with Mr. Thomas is at eleven."

"That's right," Shay said evenly. His voice was as pleasant as that of the man he faced but, in the far background, there was a difference between them; a lack of something once called breeding, or, at least, education. The clipboard user had it; Shay did not.

There had been no obvious signal, no button pressed, but the door opened behind them and a newcomer stepped out. If the first two of these mildish, polite young men looked like twins, the newcomer made it triplets.

The clipboard man said, without turning, "George, could you see Mr. Shay, here, to Mr. Thomas' office?"

"Right this way, Mr. Shay."

John Shay followed him into the building.

It lost all resemblance to a southern plantation, once inside, and took on the attributes of a modern office building, albeit with rather high ceilings. The little furniture of the small entrada and the hall beyond, which they took, was uncomfortably stiff and unutilized in appearance, consisting exclusively of straight chairs and small tables, sometimes bearing publications as bland as a vaseline sandwich. The wall-to-wall carpeting was battleship gray. Wall decorations were limited to portraits of the past five presidents, various other political-looking types, only two

of which John Shay recognized, one of them being J.
Edgar Hoover in his latter years, that G-Man of half a
century ago. There were also a general or two, an admiral
or two, looking severe and too elderly to have been on
active duty when the portraits were taken.

John Shay noted such features from the sides of his
eyes, recording all, missing nothing. He followed his es-
cort without speaking.

They wound up, eventually, at a pair of heavy wooden
double doors, after having passed a half dozen rooms with
closed portals, behind which could be made out the sounds
of office activity, including the chatter of auto-typers and
business machines. Before the door was another of the
conservatively dressed young men.

This one was cold of eye and a shade more supercilious
of expression than the others.

John Shay's guide said, "Mr. Shay, on appointment."

The new one looked at John Shay without speaking.
Shay sighed and brought forth his wallet and extended his
credentials again. The other examined them carefully, then
went through the rest of the papers the wallet contained,
quickly, efficiently.

John Shay looked at him, his lips infinitesimally paler.
Infinitesimally, but the other caught it. He handed the
wallet back and, when Shay had returned it to his pocket,
stepped suddenly forward and ran his hands over the visitor's
person in a quick frisk. Shay stood as motionless as a coiled
cottonmouth when the young man's hand darted below
Shay's left shoulder to emerge with a .38 plastic Noiseless
built onto a light frame.

The other's nostrils went up in not quite a sneer and he
said, "Naughty, naughty." He looked down at the altered
gun. Its front sight and the forepart of the trigger guard

had been filed off, and the barrel was less than two inches in length. A quick draw, vicious-looking weapon.

John Shay's hands struck in a blur. There was a chopping, a grasping, and suddenly his gun was back in his possession.

The superior one goggled. Shay's guide said nothing, but there was the slightest hint of amusement back in his eyes.

The door guard stuttered indignantly, ''You can't go into the Director's office armed!''

John Shay said coldly, ''Why didn't you just say so and ask for it?'' He reversed the gun and handed it over, and turned his eyes to the door expectantly.

The other's eyes shifted over to the newcomer's guide and quickly away again. He was no longer the cultivated gentleman, and had lost face. He snarled, ''Perhaps we'll meet again.''

Shay looked at him. ''You'd be crazy to look forward to it,'' he said, his lips barely moving with his words.

The other, fuming, ran a hand over a small electronic eye on the door's surface and stood to one side as the portal opened smoothly.

John Shay walked through.

It was the largest office he had ever seen, and the most sterile. Save for bookshelves and dark green steel files, its furniture consisted solely of a half acre of desk at the far end of the room. Shay had never heard of Mussolini and his famous office in which the visitor had to walk self-consciously, awkwardly, for endless paces before confronting the dictator, who sat there silently until his visitor had made the pilgrimage. It was a disconcerting gambit.

And bothered John Shay not at all. He strode to the desk and looked down at the man behind it, without expression. The desk was bare, without even a TV phone.

Shay said, ''Roy Thomas?''

The other took him in for a long, deliberate moment.

In some manner he must have given a signal, since a door to one side opened. Still another of the efficient gentleman types came through it bearing a straight chair which he placed before the desk, then turned and left without words.

Roy Thomas said, "Sit down."

This is the way Roy Thomas looked: A heavyset man, his body weight was copied by his square-jawed face. A bulldog face that held no amiability. A face that must have taken the better part of half a century to have achieved this hardness. He was expensively suited, as though he had departed his valet but a few moments before. His hands, which were on the desk before him, were beautifully manicured, inappropriately so, considering the short fingers—the fingers of a laborer, perhaps a miner. He looked like John L. Lewis during the days when that worthy was slugging himself to the command of the United Mine Workers. A John L. Lewis, then, but one spotlessly turned out.

John Shay sat silently and continued to await his cue.

Roy Thomas, Director of the Division of Clandestine Services, of the Inter-American Bureau of Investigation, said, "Do you know who I am?"

"Yes," Shay said, permitting no sense whatsoever of being impressed. The man before him was so hush-hush that even most news commentators of the muckraking variety were barely acquainted with his name. Indeed, there were some who were willing to debate whether or not his office existed, or whether it was a romantic invention of Greater Washington gossips.

John Shay crossed his legs.

The older man reached down and a drawer to his right

side automatically opened without his touching it. He reached inside and came up with a small sheaf of papers. He put them on the desk surface and slowly leafed through them, pausing at the second page long enough to give it a fairly good scanning.

He looked up finally and said, "You're currently going under the name of John Shay. Where did you acquire your identity papers?"

Shay shrugged.

Thomas brushed it aside. "Actually, we already know," he growled. He looked into the other's face. "John . . . Shay. The last of the hit men."

His visitor said nothing to that, either.

The Director heaved a grunt from his belly and said, "Perhaps I should say, the last of the *free-lance* hit men."

Shay said, "How'd you know how to get in touch with me?" His eyes were empty as he added, "I'm retired."

The Director of the Bureau of Investigation's Clandestine Services Division grunted again. "You don't retire in your line . . . Shay. They don't let you. We got in touch with you through some of our . . . contacts. We have a rather complete dossier on you, of course, but ordinarily your . . . activities do not come under our jurisdiction, nor even our interest. Let me congratulate you on that. However, we maintain contacts with higher echelon members of the, ah, Syndicate. What is the more popular name these days when all is more decorous and supposedly legal?" He had an irritating mannerism of pausing in the middle of a sentence, as though his next words would be particularly impressive.

Shay said flatly, "What do you want with me?"

"We wish you to perform a service, ah, in line with your field of endeavor."

The younger man took him in for a long, silent, pregnant moment and then said finally, "I thought your outfit had its own men."

The ultra-secret bureaucrat nodded his heavy head, the jowls shaking just slightly. "We can't take any chance whatever of it being traced back to this division. As you are perhaps aware, we operate under top-security conditions, but this goes even beyond that."

Shay didn't equivocate. "You want me to hit somebody?"

"Obviously. But under extraordinarily unique conditions."

The professional assassin made no attempt to hide his skepticism. "What's in it for me, supposing that you don't finish me off after I've done your dirty work?"

Thomas shook a stubby hand in an irritated brushing-off gesture. "Your personal safety is guaranteed."

Shay's expression didn't change. He had not survived in his chosen field by ever completely trusting his employers, though he numbered among them various comparatively close relatives. He had no friends. Had he had any, he wouldn't have trusted them where his profession was concerned.

The bureaucrat went on. "Very well. On completion of your assignment, you will leave this country as soon as possible. You will be given a trust fund, through Switzerland, the income from which will enable you to live at a considerably higher standard than you enjoy today. You will be forbidden ever to return to the United States of the Americas. If you do, Shay, your life will be forfeit."

"I don't like this. What happens if I don't take the job?"

Roy Thomas looked at him heavily.

Shay sighed and shrugged in rejection. "You don't roach me. I've had to go on the run before. I've got contacts that'll take care of me."

Thomas shook his head. "No, you haven't. None that count when this department is involved. Don't play Russian roulette with a single barrel shotgun, John Shay. There is no hiding, ultimately, from the Division of Clandestine Services. We have dealt, in our time, with some of the most security-minded persons in the world. Their efforts did not avail them. Your so-called contacts are under my thumb, or, at least, their superiors are. A word to the Syndicate from me would immediately be acted upon—if my own men did not get to you first."

Shay's face was characteristically expressionless but he said, "Who do you want me to hit? And how? And even . . . why? The more I know, the better I can operate."

"We don't know the name he's using."

For the first time since the interview had begun there was expression on John Shay's face. It was one of disbelief. "Don't know his name?"

Chapter Four

Ron and Zack were milking the goats in the courtyard of The Barn, the third and largest of the underground buildings of the family's complex. It not only housed an uncounted number of chickens, ducks, turkeys, geese, guinea fowl, one buck goat, eight does, anywhere from five to fifteen kids and three riding horses, but from time to time other animals including, once, a warthog which Colleen, the family animal lover, had rescued from a defunct circus during a trip in Mexico. The Barn was also their storage area for everything from hay and grain, to preserved fruits, vegetables and honey. It housed their cider press, a still, and racks for the bottles and casks which held their sweet cider, hard cider, applejack and apricot and peach brandy. There was also a room for separating milk, making buttermilk and yogurt as well as cheese. The Barn also boasted a sizable tool room and a handicraft area, complete with looms, two potter's wheels, an electric furnace, a small forge and various other equipment, most of it currently covered with dust until the spirit moved this family member or that to utilize it again—if ever.

They were milking Deera. The other goats were lined up, as always at milking time, by seniority, a system that Novie, the herd smartass, alone tried to beat. She'd invariably attempt to horn in further up the line than was her privilege, whereupon, just as invariably, her seniors would butt her back into place.

The way they milked was this: Zack would get a one-pound can of barley, which they bought by the hundred weight in Coronado, place it before the goat being milked, and then squat behind her and hold her back legs. Ron, squatting to one side, would milk the small teats of the Toggenberg into a milk bucket until the barley had been consumed, at which point the goat would rebel, wishing to reserve the rest of her milk supply for her kids. Then it'd be the turn of the next one. During this, Thor, the pedigreed buck, with a lineage longer than the Hapsburgs, would stand off to one side chewing his cud and surveying all procedures. He kept a goatish eye on everything pertaining to his harem. In his pecking order there must be no stray peckers.

Zack said, "Why'n the hell don't we have a cow or two, instead of these stinking goats?"

Zack looked like this: At twenty-six he was on the shortish side, was as ugly as a monkey and resembled the third face down on a tippler's totem pole. Nevertheless, he was the family dreamer and came up with more gimmick ideas, all of them unworkable, in an hour than the rest of the family put together did in a week. He looked like Mickey Rooney back when that energetic lad was doing musical things with Judy Garland.

Ron said, "First, per pound of animal and per pound of feed, they yield more milk than a cow and you don't have to avoid dookey doilies all over the pasture. Second, the milk is naturally homogenized." He continued to squirt the patiently chomping Deera's foaming juice into the bucket. "But third is most important of all."

"Third?" Zack said, bringing another can of feed so that Hornikins could take over from Deera.

"Yep," Ron said, first rubbing the new udder and then grabbing the next set of tits. "The herd was given us for free by the Roskin family when they gave up soul-farming and headed for Alaska."

Ron looked like this: Although he was a brother, or half-brother, of Zack (they didn't know which), there was no family resemblance. Ron was slight, delicate of bone structure, aristocratic of appearance in the English gentleman tradition. He was one year older than Zack and blondish, rather than dark. Colleen might be the animal lover of the family but it was Ron the animals followed around emanating affection. His voice was soft and he seldom argued, even at family councils. He looked like Leslie Howard playing Henry Higgins in *Pygmalion*.

Zack grunted and said, "How's the novel coming?" He strengthened his grip on Hornikins's legs; Hornikins was inclined to stick a foot in the milk pail, given the chance.

"I've temporarily given it up," Ron admitted. "The best way of breaking into writing is doing poetry. Poetry with a message."

"Poetry," Zack snorted. "Who the hell reads poetry anymore?"

"People with sensitivity," Ron told him.

"Oh," his brother said. "So let's hear some of your sensitive poetry you're going to floor them with."

Ron ignored the sarcasm and said, "Listen to this. I wrote it last night. The title is, *Quis custodiet ipsos custodes?*"

Zack looked over at him and scowled in disbelief. "It's what?"

"That's from some old Roman. It means, 'Who's to Watch Over the Watchers?' The poem goes like this:

"Who's to watch over the watchers,
"Those who would carry the lashes?
"What was that tune that Joshua played?
"Who hauls the janitor's ashes?"

Zack almost loosened his grip on Hornikins as he stared. "What in the hell's that supposed to mean?" he demanded.

Ron was as indignant as his nature allowed him, which wasn't very. He said plaintively, "Don't you see? It's an answer to those cloddies in Greater Washington who are trying to compile this Revised Constitution. Some of them claim that we should go through a period of at least five years under a benevolent dictatorship. For five years, a dictatorship would run the country, until they've smoothed over all the confusion. So the question is, if they're going to watch over us, who's going to be watching over them? It's an unanswerable question, like asking what tune Joshua's army played when they marched around Jericho making with its brass orchestra."

Zack shook his head in resignation. "It'll never sell. I can see that if this family ever makes any money beyond our GAS it'll have to come from me."

Ron said, "Yeah? How're you doing with those ideas you submit to the novelty company?"

Zack radiated enthusiasm. "Sooner or later, I'll make it, Ron. It's a natural. I've got a million ideas. Come up with just one new novelty gimmick and you're rich. A game, a fad, a new gizmo that everybody'll buy. The novelty business is one they'll never be able to automate and computerize. And anybody can get rich in it. All you need is the right idea."

Ron said skeptically, "What'd they say about that gimmick idea you had last month? The rubber crutch you give to cripples you don't like?"

Zack's face fell. "They said it was old hat, it's already been done. Also black water, that's been done too."

Ron's face came up from his task and he looked at the other blankly. "Black water?" he said. "Its possible use seems to elude me."

"Yeah, yeah. For people to wash with who don't care if they're clean or not."

Ron closed his eyes and inwardly called for greater strength, and returned to his milking.

Zack said, "They rejected that but it gave me a new idea. Colored water for pet fish—goldfish and so forth. You'd have to come up with some kind of dye that wouldn't hurt the fish. All different colors, pink, blue, green, violet. You could change the color of the water your pet fish swims in according to your color scheme of the day, or according to your mood. Or maybe according to the fish's mood. Suppose one or the other of you're feeling lousy. Blue water in the goldfish bowl."

"Oh, come on, Zack," his brother protested. "Who in the hell'd buy colored water for pet fish?"

But Zack's enthusiasm couldn't be squelched. He said, "I tell you, people will buy anything—absolutely, positively *anything*—if it's the fad. I was just reading the other day about a camp fad back in the 1970s. Pet rocks. Some advertising man named Gary Dahl dreamt it up. They sold by the hundreds of thousands through even big department stores like Neiman-Marcus and Macy's. They were just ordinary pink rocks. With each one came a manual, *Care and Training of Your Pet Rock*. The instructions said that pet rocks needed no lessons to be able to sit, play dead or roll over, especially downhill.''

Ron was ogling him. ''You've got to be kidding.''

''No. I tell you, people will buy anything if it seems novel, especially if they think everybody *else* is buying it too. Anything. Sooner or later, I'll come up with one that'll hit. I'm working on a natural. *Cosmetics For Canines*. It's never been properly exploited.''

''Cosmetics. Canines?'' Ron said weakly.

''A natural. All those silly broads who go ape over their poodles, cockers, pekingese and so forth. Doggy shampoos, doggy perfumes, both female and male. Manicure sets, including various shaded claw polish, curling irons especially for dogs, even eye make-up. Rinses and so forth in case you want to change the color of its hair, maybe to match your own. Uh—doggy douche, maybe.''

Ron said bitterly, ''How about cosmetic surgery? Face lifting for Boxers and Bulldogs?''

''Golly,'' Zack said. ''You're getting the idea.''

Ron stood up. ''Come on,'' he said. ''Let's put this milk in the reefer and go get something to eat.''

They put the milk away—leaving it for whoever the spirit moved, most likely Blackie or JoJo, to see to such matters as separating it, making butter, buttermilk, yogurt or cheese—and headed for the main dwelling. If the spirit didn't move anybody, the milk would undoubtedly go sour—a boon to the pigs, who weren't choosy.

Going back to an earlier subject, Ron said, as they walked, ''Besides, cows are stupid, goats are smart. If a cow was in a stall in a wooden barn and the barn started to burn, it wouldn't kick the stall down and escape. It'd stand there and moo until it was medium rare.''

"What'd the goat do?" Zack said.

"Probably piss on the fire."

They entered the underground house by way of the garage entrance, built into the side of the hill, the door camouflaged so that one had to be quite near before the door could be seen. From even a comparatively short distance, it looked like a natural area in boulders, interspaced with clumps of sage.

They went on through into the patio and then into the saloon. The only occupants were Bitter Joe, the Doc and a stranger. The stranger was a Negro. He and Bitter Joe were sitting to one side talking while Doc, the family gourmet, chef and food buff in general, was setting up the main table for the usual evening smorgasbord. Already available for the onslaught of man, woman and child were such items as corned beef and corned tongue, cold chicken in various forms, pâtés, chopped liver, a large baked bass, a multitude of various types of pickles, and a couple of bowls of fruit, mostly apples, apricots and peaches. Doc was bringing in more, a wide selection of salads.

As Ron and Zack entered, Bitter Joe was saying to the stranger, "You know, there's something about all blacks. You've all got it."

The newcomer's face changed only infinitesimally. "What's that?" he said mildly. He looked hefty enough to break Bitter Joe in half.

The stranger looked like this: He hadn't gone completely to flab but he obviously no longer did pushups in the morning. He was about six feet and in his day probably walked around with the grace of a tiger, but this was no longer quite his day. He was in his mid-thirties or so, and had very short, kinky hair, Caucasian features rather than Negroid ones, and was shaded about like the average American Indian. He might have been strikingly handsome back in his twenties and was still good-looking. He was dressed indolently, casually, and obviously for comfort. He looked quite a bit like that singer-actor of yesteryear, Harry Belafonte.

"Dark complexion," Bitter Joe told him reasonably. "You've all got dark complexions."

The newcomer broke up. His laugh was good.

Bitter Joe said to Zack and Ron, "Meet Moon. Franny brought him around. She's come back. Don't know for how long."

Moon stood and grinned as they shook hands and Zack said, "Moon?"

The newcomer said in easy self-deprecation, "My mother's last name was Mullins. Somehow or other, I can't escape from Moon. People who don't even know me start calling me that. There used to be an old comic strip called Moon Mullins."

Doc came back in from the kitchen and said, "Why don't you two get washed up and come on back for a quick drink before the thundering herd stampedes?"

Ron and Zack left, heading for the community bathroom.

Moon sank back into his chair again and took up the amber colored glass he'd been supplied with.

"So you're prejudiced," he smiled at Bitter Joe.

"That's right," Bitter Joe told him, picking up his own glass. "In this family, we hate all categories, no matter what race, creed, color, or nationality."

"Except WASPs?"

"Especially WASPs," Bitter Joe said very sincerely. "They got so many categories to be hated in. But also all people in conglomerate groupings, such as Whites, Blacks, Reds, Browns, Yellows, the whole shebang of colors. Also Americans, French, Russians, Chinese and so forth. Also Christians, Moslems, Jews, Buddhists, Pagans and so on. We even hate atheists and agnostics. The only people we like are individuals. It's simple; we only hate people when you start grouping them up.''

Moon was laughing. ''I'm beginning to feel at home,'' he said.

''Right,'' Doc said, re-entering with still more dishes from the kitchen, this time various breads from corn pone to pumpernickel. ''You know, you start off with a lot in your favor, Moon. Franny brought you. Franny's one of ours.''

''That's what she told me,'' Moon said, taking a sip of his drink. ''Holy smokes, this is the best hard cider I've ever wrapped a lip around. Tastes like champagne. You don't make it yourself?''

Doc said, pretending indignation, ''You think we'd poison ourselves with commercial stuff? We make all of our own drinkables. We don't swill carbonated urine.''

Doc looked like this: Somewhere in his early forties, he gave the impression of not giving a damn save for food. Fat almost to the point of being blubbery, he obviously didn't care about his physical appearance. He wore his short hair like Napoleon, when it was combed at all, and since he seldom wore anything but shorts and sandals, weather permitting, Doc boasted the darkest tan in the family. In spite of his heft, he moved energetically, especially about the kitchen, or working in the guzzle department over in The Barn. His face had a cherub's cheerful innocence. In fact, Doc looked something like Truman Capote.

He went back into the kitchen for more dishes.

The Twins and Ruthie came bustling in, followed by the Wizard at a more dignified pace. They all four ignored the stranger, swiped some freshly baked brownies from the table and retired with them to a far corner of the room before anyone could say them nay. Not that Bitter Joe was about to do so. He cherished the theory that if they'd kill their appetites with preliminary sweets, there was a chance of something being left of the buffet for the adults.

Moon said, "That's a fine-looking spread. Franny said you raised most of your own food yourselves."

"That's right," Bitter Joe snorted. "One reason the family moved out here was to avoid gook food, processed food, frozen food, commercially canned food, supposedly fresh fruits and vegetables shipped green, and all the rest of it. Americans are both the most fed *and* the worst fed people in the civilized world."

Moon finished his drink and said mildly, "They think they're the *best* fed. You mean you even make your own sausages? Some of those are mighty professional looking."

"We stuff our own. But we have to use goat intestines, instead of sheep, which are supposed to be best."

Rusty and Sweet Alice came in through one door, the Professor through another. Moon stood and Bitter Joe introduced them. Sweet Alice ran her eyes up and down the newcomer's build appreciatively. Moon blinked.

Rusty smiled her wry, honest smile while shaking hands and said, "Where's Franny?"

"In town, I think," Moon said. "She had some business or other she had to take care of. We drove through Coronado on the way out here. Looks fifty years out of date."

"At least," Rusty said. "The last of the 19th century

small towns. The people go with it. Time's passed them by.''

Doc came in at the same time Ron and Zack re-entered and said, putting a last three or four dishes on the table, ''Let's go folks. Grab a plate, Moon. Try those mushrooms.''

''Yeah. You try them first, Moon,'' Bitter Joe said. ''The kids picked them. As a stranger, you're expendable.''

Moon grinned and they all set to, the youngsters coming a-running.

Doc said, ''Where's Blackie?''

''I think she had some shopping. She went in with Franny,'' the Professor told him. His plate was full and he found a chair and said to Moon, ''You on your way through, or can you stay awhile?''

''Just looking around for a place to settle,'' Moon said, finding a chair of his own. ''I've been traveling around a lot ever since the computers bounced me out of my job. But I'm getting tired of it. Franny suggested I give you folks a look.''

''Great,'' Rusty said, spearing some cold goose and shoveling sliced pickles onto her plate. ''You on GAS?''

''That's right. I had a pretty good job for awhile. Thought I was all set. But now it's Guaranteed Annual Stipend, along with just about everybody else.''

''Ummm,'' Doc said, eating away at the mushroom dish he had recommended. ''I never got to practice in my profession at all. Tenth in my class but medicine is so computerized these days, you know, I never got an appointment. What did you do, Moon?''

Most of them were settled down now.

Moon said, ''Biologist. Research biologist.''

"That so?" the Professor said, around a corned beef sandwich. "What field were you in?"

"Animals," Moon told him. "Mostly chimpanzees, hamsters and dogs. That reminds me."

He looked over into a corner. The newcomers to the Saloon hadn't noticed the small black dog there. He had evidently conked out, tired of the trip he'd just gone through with Moon and Franny.

Moon said, "Hungry, Bowser?"

One end of the mound of frowzy, black, curly hair came up. The other end seemed to give some kind of a wag, though through the hair you couldn't make out a tail.

Bowser looked like this: He was about the size of a cocker but looked like a rather dirty-black miniature sheep dog. That is, he had lots of hair. *Lots* of it. If he stood still, or was recumbent, it was hard to tell which end was wag and which was bite, unless he stuck his black nose out, or unless you noticed the tips of his ears. He didn't really look like any other dog that ever was.

"Yeah," a voice said.

Moon looked at the Doc, who was obviously in charge of the family kitchen, at least for this meal. He said, "You have anything I could give Bowser?"

"Ummm, sure." The Doc made a hospitable flowing gesture with a beefy hand at the table. "Anything. We don't have any dogs on the place right now, so we don't have any special dog food."

Moon looked over at the black tangle of hair. "You hear that, Bowser?"

And the dog said, "Then I guess I'll have a sausage."

Silence fell.

Chapter Five

Moon said, "Fine," and got up from his chair, went over and picked up a bowl, put one of the large-size pork sausages in it, and took it over and placed it in front of the dog.

Bowser said, "Jesus, that smells good," and grabbed it up.

Moon went back to his chair, took up his own plate again, and resumed work on his paté, pumpernickel, home pickled beets and salad. He said to the Professor, "I had about four years in research in all. Fascinating work."

Rusty came to her feet and took up a pitcher. The rest of the family adults were staring, motionless, at the eloquent Bowser. She said weakly, "Christ, we'd better have a little more of this cider, Moon."

Ron blurted, "He talked!" He was staring accusingly at the family's guest.

Moon looked up at him and said around his mouthful of food, "Eh?"

"The dog," Ron said accusingly. "He talked."

"Oh. Oh, yes. I was telling you about it. He's the best specimen I worked on. Of course, he started off with an advantage. He's a Sazarac."

Zack, who was bug-eyeing the dog in question, said, "He's what? I heard him talk too."

"A Sazarac," Moon said. "Sazarac terrier. You've probably heard of them. Atlas Mountains, in Morocco. Bred 'em for intelligence, since God only knows when. Before the Carthaginians ever got to Tingis. They call it Tangier now. One of the oldest cities in the world. I lived in Tangier for, oh, a year or so. It's the damnedest town you ever . . ."

"Wait a minute," Doc demanded. "You mean to say that overhaired dog can talk?"

"Bowser?" Moon said, stuffing his mouth again.

At the mention of his name, one end of Bowser came up. He had finished his sausage. There was a suspicious movement at his other end, possibly where a cropped tail was located.

The Wizard and Ruthie had come up now, as well, and were staring at the little dog as blankly as the adult members of the family. The Twins went on gobbling the unlikely selection of food they had chosen, mostly desserts. They obviously didn't give a damn about talking dogs. Possibly it hadn't occured to them that all dogs didn't.

"Ummm, Bowser," the Doc said, his voice halfway between being ominous and cold. "It sounded as though he answered you."

Moon frowned and waved a fork gently in explanation. "I was telling you about it. I'm a research biologist. At least I was before I was bounced by the computers. I tell you, those God-damned data banks don't give you a Chinaman's chance—even a black Chinaman. Here I had my schooling, top honors, at John Hopkins University City, and four years on the job. And what happened? They grabbed me by the scruff of the ass and tossed me out that fast.''

He got up and went back to the spread on the table and looked at it judiciously, fork in hand.

Nobody else was eating. Half of them were staring at Bowser, half at the self-proclaimed biologist.

Zack, his monkey face impatient, said, ''The dog, the dog. He talked.''

''Oh. Oh, yeah. Well, we altered his voice box, of course. But the important thing was the I.Q. Except for the dolphin work—I've never been in on that, but that's where the *real* action is—except for the dolphins you've got to simultaneously work on the I.Q. or you've got nothing. Hamsters, for instance. You take hamsters . . .''

''The dog,'' Rusty said. ''Christ. Take the damned pooch.''

Moon looked at her reproachfully. ''Don't talk like that. How'd you like him to call you a damned human broad?''

''Christ, I'd love it,'' Rusty muttered. ''I'd love to have him say anything more. I haven't had a drop to drink.'' That reminded her and she got up and went over to the bar and poured herself a sustaining double slug of applejack.

Which, in turn, reminded Doc of something. After all, he was the host, so to speak. He'd made the spread this evening. He looked over at the unlikely pile of dirty black hair and said, ''Would you like something else, Bowser?''

And Bowser said, ''Oh, I'll have another sausage.''

Doc took up another sausage in his plump fingers,

thought secondly about that, put it back and speared it more hygienically with a fork before carrying it over to Bowser's plate.

Bowser grabbed it, while the family looked on in fascination. When he'd polished it off, he said, "Jesus. That's swell sausage."

"Ummm, it's homemade," Doc said emptily, staring down at him.

"You can tell," Bowser said in appreciation. He stretched out once more.

Moon said, "He's pooped. We've been driving all day. Uh, where was I going to sleep tonight? I'll tuck him in."

Ron said, "You can have my room. I'll sleep with Colleen or Sweet Alice."

Moon blinked at that cavalier statement but took up the dog and followed the younger man out into the patio and toward the other's bedroom .

Behind him, in the saloon, Zack said, heading for the bar where he sloshed applejack into a tumbler, "Golly, a talking mutt."

Rusty said, "I still don't believe it."

Moon and Ron came back and the newcomer took up his plate and returned to his food with satisfaction.

The Professor cleared his throat and said, "Uh, this, uh, talking dog. How is it that we haven't heard about it on the newscasts, or read about it?"

Moon shook a fork at them as he chewed away. "There's been a lot about it in the professional scientific journals, especially pertaining to dolphins. The idea was to use them as kind of deep-sea cowboys. Supervise the new herds of meat whales."

The Wizard said, "Now that you mention it, I ran into some discussion of upgrading the chimpanzee's intelligence and giving him a voice box, so we could use them for laboring jobs.''

Moon nodded and took a gulp of his hard cider to wash down some of the food. "Yeah, that was a project for awhile. But we don't need common laborers much any more. Practically every job going is automated. Besides, it's a bastard to work with chimps. They're hysterical.''

"Yes, of course," the Professor said. "It does seem to me that I've read bits and pieces about altering the DNA of animals so as to change their basic characteristics. But I didn't know it had gone this far.''

Moon twisted his mouth a little. "It's been a bit hush-hush. Some of the crackpot element, you know, the SPCA and such, get all excited about our working on animals. So we've avoided too much publicity. I got into it since my specializations were gene deletion, gene insertion and gene surgery.''

They all looked properly blank. Two or three of them helped themselves to more food, but all eyes were on Moon.

He said, shaking his fork once again, "The microsurgery of DNA can be achieved by physical methods; fine beams of radiation, such as lasers or pulsed x-rays, to slice through the DNA molecule at desired points, or to knock out small sections, so as to eliminate specific defects. Alternately, repressor molecules have been found which can be introduced to block the expression of particular characteristics in a precise manner. We definitely know that certain molecules are so shaped that they can embed themselves between the projections of the DNA chain. That's how repressor molecules work.''

Zack said plaintively, "Golly, what the hell's all that mean? What about this talking dog?''

The Wizard said impatiently, staring at Moon through his heavy rimmed glasses, "Shut up. Go on, Moon."

Moon said, "Well, that's about it. We also use viruses to carry information into the cell. But copying desired DNAs or even the synthesis of DNA to a desired pattern eliminates the need for such detailed tinkering. You probably all know that many years back, we constructed in the laboratory molecules of the nucleic acid types, capable of assembling amino acids into protein-like structures."

The Doc said, "You know, I can understand about every other word of all this. Three more glasses of apple-jack and I'll understand all of it."

Moon said plaintively, rubbing a dark hand back over his short hair, "The trouble with science, these days, is that it's so hellishly specialized that you can't talk to anybody, no matter how you try to simplify, unless he's in your own field."

Rusty shook her head and said, "Great. But what you've done with, uh, Bowser is give him a voice box, whatever that is, and upped his intelligence, eh?"

Their visitor beamed at her. "That's exactly right."

Zack said, "Well, if you've got the technique all down pat, why not do it to all dogs?"

Moon looked at him sarcastically. "See here, friend. Down through the ages man has had the dog. Man's best friend. You know why he was man's best friend? Because he couldn't talk and he was so dumb that no matter what his human master did, the dog thought it was fine. How would you like to have a pooch that was jabbering at you all day, instead of just wagging its tail, and just smart enough to realize the stupidity of some of the things you customarily did? Might as well have a teenager . . ."

Blackie came in, bearing a couple of packages, and

said, "Hello, everybody. I see that you waited for me, in a pig's ass. Hi, Moon. How do you take to the family?"

"Fine, so far," Moon said, sighing and putting his now empty plate down on the central table. "And I hope that the feeling's reciprocal."

Blackie put her purchases on a chair and went about the table filling a plate. She said to Moon, "Franny's still in town. Why don't we all gather around and have a family council? You can ask any damn questions you want and we'll fill you in. Franny thinks you'd be a great addition to our group."

Rusty and Sweet Alice began clearing off the table, taking dirty dishes and utensils and now largely emptied serving dishes back to the kitchen. The Twins and Ruthie snagged another supply of the brownies while the going was good. Doc, the Professor, Ron and Zack went over to the bar and selected fruit liqueurs. Doc poured a hefty jolt out of one bottle into a snifter glass and brought it over to their guest.

"Try this," he said. "Apricot brandy. Distilled down to the point where there's hardly any sweet left in it. The Hungarians call it Barack."

Blackie, eating away, found a comfortable chair and sank into it with the wheeze of the late middle-aged. She said to Moon, "All right, fire away on anything you want to know about the family."

Blackie looked like this: Though a bit heavy-set, she didn't seem her sixty years. The ranking feminine member of the Chutzpa family, she still projected, through her matronly air the vivacious girl she must have once been. Not even her figure was completely gone, and her hair, now heavily streaked with gray, still gave indication of the once jet black which had yielded her nickname. The wrinkles of her face were minimal and largely laugh wrinkles at the sides of eyes and mouth. She looked like a matronly Shirley MacLaine at, say, fifty-five.

"Now, wait a minute," Zack said urgently. "About this dog. Golly, are there many of them?"

Moon frowned and said, "No, not many. I took the best specimen. The only Sazarac. Then the Department of Scientific Research killed the appropriation for everything but the dolphins. And a dolphin won't chase cats, or bring your pipe and slippers. Hell, at the rate they're going there won't be any more scientific research at all. They don't want progress, the bastards. They're afraid it might upset their applecart."

Zack was leaning forward in his chair. "Do they breed true? I mean, after you've altered the DNA, or whatever you called it, and all?"

Moon scowled and thought about it. "Well, not really. We didn't carry that aspect through. Did hardly anything on it at all." He thought about it some more. "If you got another Sazarac and bred her to Bowser and she had, say, eight pups, possibly not more than half would be like Bowser. Two of the others would probably be smarter than usual, and the other two might be able to talk, at least a little." He thought about it still more. Then, "Of course, if you bred Bowser back to one of his daughters, one of those most like him, or bred the pups back to each other, except those that didn't come through, you'd probably, sooner or later, be breeding them true."

Zack said, "How'd you get another Sazarac to breed him to?"

Moon said, "Oh, that wouldn't be any problem. They've never become popular like poodles or police dogs, but they're available. Any place that deals in pets could order you one.''

Blackie said, looking back and forth between them, ''What in the devil's all this crap about?''

Doc said, after clearing his throat, ''Moon's got one helluva dog.''

''Well, great, dammit, but let's get on with the family council,'' she said. She looked over at Moon again. ''Any questions about our set-up here?''

The big man took a sip of his brandy, made pursed lips indicating approval of it, and said, ''As a matter of fact, Franny gave me a quick drive around, and part of the story. Very impressive. All your buildings underground and all.''

The Professor said, ''Yes, of course. We follow the Malcolm B. Wells conception of architecture. He taught that all animals' lives utterly depend upon living green plants. That plants alone give us our food; they alone renew and refresh the air, they alone recycle organic wastes, and they alone store sunlight for our use. Obviously, the plants must have ground space on which to live, but our buildings and roads were using up ground space at a suicidal rate. Therefore, those of us who were building and paving were helping to plunge the planet into disaster. Good grief, it's as simple as that; the architects, engineers, realtors, developers, planners, builders and pavers who are destroyers of that plant life are public enemies. So we built all of our buildings underground, with a maximum of plants, even trees, growing on the tops and the sides.''

Rusty nodded support. ''Christ, yes. We believe that all buildings—most of which are eyesores anyway—and roads should be underground. It's practical too. Nice and cool in the summer, like caves, and easy to heat in the winter.''

"Makes sense," Moon admitted. "But how'd you finance all of this?"

Blackie, who alone was still eating, said, her voice matronly, "No trouble there. There's seven of us collecting GAS and one working, Colleen. Everything goes into the family kitty. You haven't met Colleen, yet. She's still in town on her job. Perhaps Franny will drive her home."

"That reminds me," Rusty said. "JoJo should go in and register for her GAS. She ought to be eighteen now."

Moon said, "Wait a minute, now. You pool all of your pseudo-dollar credits. Fine. But how do you decide who spends what?"

Blackie frowned at him. "Hell, anyone spends anything he wants to spend. You see, we've all legally changed our last names to Chutzpa, and have a family account with the National Data Bank Banking Section. And all adults have a Universal Credit Card. Actually, the way we live, we've usually got a surplus. If some major expenditure comes up we sometimes have a family council to discuss it."

"Sometimes?" Moon said in protest. "You mean, in actuality, any one of you, on his own, could spend your bank holdings, your savings and all? Just like that, without consulting anybody else?"

Blackie looked at him as though nothing could be more reasonable. "Why not? What in the hell would he, or she, spend it on?"

"But you can't conduct an enterprise that way. This is a fairly major project. Why, it must have cost tens of thousands for the land and . . ."

"Ummm," Doc said. "But we homesteaded it, you know. There's still lots of this kind of land that's government-owned. You should have seen it before we started developing."

"Yes," Moon said desperately. "But all the buildings and equipment and furniture and everything."

Rusty said, "We built most of it ourselves. What we didn't know how to do, or what we couldn't make ourselves, like glass for the windows and all, we used our family credits on. We even got a bulldozer in for digging."

Something came to Moon. He looked at Blackie suspiciously and said, "Fine, but look, who owns all this?"

And she looked back and said reasonably again, "Why, nobody, dear."

Doc said, "Ummm. Well, actually, I guess you'd say the whole family does."

"But look. Franny suggested that I join up with you. If I did, then I'd legally change my name to Chutzpa, get a Universal Credit Card in that name and then be able to draw on the family funds and I'd be part owner?"

"Of course," Ron said, his tone asking what the new-comer was getting at.

Moon took a deep breath and plunged on. "You raise all your own food?"

Blackie said, "Oh, hell no. There's lots of things we have to use our GAS pseudo-dollars for. Salt, what sugar we use—we prefer honey, usually—tea, coffee. Of course, we roast and grind our own coffee, but we have to buy the green beans. Then, things like cereals; wheat, oats, barley. They aren't practical to raise on a small place. That's one time automated agriculture comes in: can't be beaten. And, of course, we have to buy tools and cloth for our clothes, or warp and yarn for the stuff we hand-loom."

That brought something else to mind. Moon said, "See here, who decides who does what work and for how long? There must be one helluva lot of work around here, doing the farming, taking care of the animals, weaving, taking care of the buildings, housework . . . and a lot of other things that don't immediately come to my mind.''

Blackie said placidly, ''Why, we all do. Usually, who-ever does it best. Doc, for instance, usually makes our hard cider and applejack and the brandy and so forth. He's a drunken ass.''

''I resemble that remark,'' Doc protested.

''But who decides?'' Moon said.

''The doer,'' Blackie told him, finishing her food and putting the plate down on the table. Ron picked it up and carried it into the kitchen.

Blackie went on. ''Any of us do anything that has to be done if the spirit moves us.''

Moon shook his head, in rejection of that. ''Suppose something comes at that has to be done and the spirit doesn't move anybody to do it?'

Sweet Alice, who didn't seem to be much of a talker (judging from her facial expression, not much of a thinker), told him brightly, ''Then it doesn't get done.''

Moon said desperately, ''But, look. Then a loafer could just sit and do nothing. And somebody else'd be doing all the work.

Bitter Joe spoke up finally. He said, ''I think I can see what you're building up to. See here, there's a lot of we extended families. Tens of thousands. Hell, I suppose hundreds of thousands of them, maybe millions, through-out the country. Most have got some kind of a theme. They've become an extended family, a group family, or whatever you want to call it, because they've got some-thing in common. Some are working on some kind of a project, some particular study or something. Some are in the arts; writers, painters, sculptors, handicraft workers, whatever. Some sell some of their products for extra pseudo-dollar credits, some live on GAS alone. Some gather together for sex reasons; homosexuals, bi-sexuals or just plain swingers in general. Some are sports fanatics in this sport or that, or a combination of them. Some specialize in fishing and hunting, outdoorsman stuff in general.''

"I know all that," Moon said. "But this family . . .''

"We like this way of life. If we didn't, we wouldn't belong to the family. We'd go somewhere else. We like to raise our own food. We like to have our own animals. If anybody wants to loaf, let 'em. But loafing on a full-time basis is a pain in the ass. We don't give a good hump about how much work *you* do. We find it fun and satisfying.''

Moon gave up, at least temporarily, that line of query. He said, "All right, I can live with that—but there's something else. Who's married to who, here?''

The faces of those around him, most of whom had settled onto couches, or had pulled up chairs, were blank again.

Doc said, "Ummm. Nobody.''

But Bitter Joe looked at Blackie and scowled. He said, "We're married, aren't we?''

Blackie frowned too and said, "I guess we are at that, dear. Hell, that was a long time ago.'' Her eyes went back to Moon and she said, "Joe and I are the two oldest members of the family. We were in it before it became an extended family. It was kind of a commune, back on the Saint John's River in Florida. About thirty of us, off and on. They came and went. Nothing permanent.''

Moon said, "But—the kids. Who do they belong to?''

And Rusty said, as though she didn't know what he was talking about, "How do you mean?''

"I mean, *who do they belong to*? Whose children are they?''

"Oh," the Professor said. "Yes, of course. I see what you mean. In the old-fashioned sort of way." He mulled it over, then said, "They belong to all of us. And, for that matter, we belong to them. Good grief, we're all one family."

"Fine, fine. But I'm a geneticist. What I mean is, well . . ." he jabbed a finger at little Ruthie, who had been taking him in, seated off to one side, in a sloe-eyed manner beyond her years. "Who's her mother?"

Rusty said vaguely, "Jeez, I guess I am."

Moon said, exasperated, "You guess? Who's the father?"

"How would I know?"

Blackie said with motherly sweetness, "I gave birth to Ron and Zack. Uh, I suppose that Joe or the Doc or the Professor was the father." She considered it. "Unless I was having an affair with some bastard outside of the family at the time. I can't remember."

"Colleen's the mother of the twins," Sweet Alice said charmingly, in her effort to help.

Moon learned fast. "Well. Who was their—uh, I withdraw the question." He ran his tongue over his underlip and said, "You don't mean that you interbreed, do you? That is, that anybody might have a child by anybody?"

Doc cleared his throat and said earnestly, "Oh, no. We adults only sleep with family members to whom we're not immediately related by blood lines."

Sweet Alice amended that by adding, "Or, at least, we're awful careful."

Moon didn't ask her what she meant by that. He switched the subject somewhat. "I'm surprised you don't have more children in the family," he said.

Rusty shrugged wryly. "Why?" she said. "Who wants more children? The birth rate's been falling in America for decades. I think it was way back in 1973 or '74 that it first fell to the point of population growth. And just in time, too. If we'd kept up increasing at the rate we were doing right after the Second World War, we'd be ass-deep in icky diapers.''

The Professor nodded to that. "Yes, of course. When I was a child everybody was predicting that we'd have over three hundred million population by the year 2000. But just because a trend exists doesn't mean it'll continue. A fertility rate of 2.11 per family is considered the replacement level, the level of fertility at which a population will replace itself under projected mortality rates and in the absence of migration in or out of the country. In America, the fertility rate fell below the replacement level in 1972 with 2.02 children per family, in 1973 with 1.9 and in 1974 with 1.86 and it's continued to fall slowly ever since.''

Moon screwed up his face. "Well, fine, but don't you think we owe it to the human race to continue perpetuating, to continue having children?''

."Why?'' Zack said. "Golly, what did the human race ever do for us?''

Blackie tried to put it better. She said, "The need for large numbers of children fell off. In fact, the population explosion was causing chaos especially in regions like India, Indonesia, Central Africa, Latin America. Millions were starving or on the verge of it, because there were just too damn many people. Then we began to face reality, with the most advanced countries coming to the natural conclusions first. I think Japan led the way, about 1970, when her fertility rate fell below the replacement level. West Germany was pretty close behind, then the Scandinavian countries and England.''

Moon said, "Then, you don't like children?"

Rusty said, wry as usual, "That's not the way to put it. We all like the children members of the family. It's just that we don't want to be swarming with them. It's something like that old saying, when the world's ready for railroads, railroads come. And when the world no longer needs children, en masse, they become undesirable. They are no longer needed as workers on the family farm, the old-style family farm, or as cheap child labor in the factories, like back in the 19th Century. So they become objectionable, so objectionable that people don't want them. They begin to criticize and become contemptuous and even to hate their parents. This began to show up shortly after the Second World War. The kids no longer obeyed, they became dropouts, they refused to even help around the house. Such little chores as washing the dishes became so abhorrent to them that they made a full-time project of fluffing off. At the same time, both parents were beginning to work, in order to keep their living standards, so they didn't have time for kids. And at the same time, houses and apartments began to get smaller and smaller, with one or two bedrooms, rather than half a dozen. And a lot of landlords wouldn't even allow children. Alakazam! The population explosion was over."

Chapter Six

Moon's slumber had been thrown off by the rather fast driving he and Franny had been doing from the eastern states to the southwest and he awoke at dawn's early light.

He lay there for awhile on his back, his hands behind his head, staring at the ceiling. This had been quite an evening. He had come in contact with extended families before. In fact, they were rapidly taking over the country, especially among the elements who depended upon Guaranteed Annual Stipend for their income. But he couldn't remember ever having run into a family quite this far-out.

He supposed that the trend had started some thirty years ago, in Denmark, when a bill to legalize group marriages had been introduced in the Folketing, the Danish parliament. And then in America in 1971 in the State of Wisconsin, when Assembly Bill 1588 was introduced by Representative Lloyd Barbee, and referred to the Committee on Judiciary. It called for up to three married couples, all age

30 or more, to enter into group marriages under nonprofit corporation laws. It exempted all persons organizing such marriages from laws prohibiting bigamy and adultery. The same Proposition 31, as it was called after a book by Robert Rimmer, was later introduced in California, after it was found that group marriage was already taking place without such laws on the books.

He had met the final two family members shortly before taking off for bed. They had been JoJo, a teenager, who had been horseback riding in the mountains, and Colleen, the one who was unique in the sense that she alone of them all had a job. JoJo had turned out to be a stunningly beautiful girl, as brunette as Sweet Alice was blonde but, happily, of higher intelligence. Colleen was unfortunately unattractive, overweight and severe, and Moon got the impression that she was impatient of the fact that none of the other family members brought in additional income as a result of working. Not that any of them seemed to give a damn about that, and obviously they would have been just as happy if Colleen, as well, had thrown up the earnest life and gone onto GAS.

Moon finally stretched, got up and looked about the room he had taken over from Ron. It was comfortable enough, moderate in size but not truly small, and the rugs and bedclothes were obviously handmade, as were the furniture, including the bedstead. Two windows and a door opened out onto the large patio of the underground building, another door into the rest of the house. The patio was a pleasure to see. Obviously, some of the Chutzpa family often had the spirit move them toward gardening efforts. Two of the largest bougainvillea he had ever seen, one red, one purplish, dominated the walls. There were worse places to live, he decided.

Bowser had made the foot of the bed his domain. Now, Moon made out the fact that the little dog had opened one eye and was watching him.

Moon said, "Morning, Bowser. You wowed them last night."

There was a stirring of what was undoubtedly the shaggy animal's cropped tail, at his other end, but for the nonce the dog remained in his comfortably warm spot.

Moon thought a moment, then went over to his oversized suitcase. It was spread out on the room's largest chair. He reached into it and came up with a light dressing gown and a pair of slippers. He got into them and looked down into the piece of luggage again, considering. He shrugged, leaned down, and fished into a small side pocket, and came up with what looked like a fountain pen. He slipped this into one of the dressing gown pockets and headed for the door to the patio. Bowser stayed pat.

There was no one in the patio at this early hour, a quick glance told him. He headed for the saloon.

There was no one in the saloon, either, nor, upon check, in the kitchen beyond.

Moon stood and listened for a long moment. He could hear nothing. Nobody seemed to be stirring. He had thought that possibly it was necessary in the early hours to milk the goats or take care of some other farm chores about the haphazardly run place, but evidently not.

He brought his little gadget from his pocket, pressed a stud on its end and started about the room, pointing it here, there, everywhere and especially in the vicinity of any electronic devices, such as the large Tri-Di screen, the TV phone, electrical outlets and lamps. The whole room took him but a few minutes and, evidently satisfied, he returned the device to his pocket and thought about it.

He looked into the kitchen for a moment, but then shook his head and, recrossing the saloon, returned via the patio to his bedroom. All the rooms in the large, rambling underground dwelling seemed to lead off the patio as well as into the interior.

Back in his room, Moon was awarded with a double wag by a still sleepy Bowser. He began to duplicate his actions in the saloon. That is, he brought forth his gadget again and directed it about, and particularly at anything involving electricity.

A voice said, "Whatcha doing?"

Moon turned quickly.

In the interior doorway stood the nine-year old, Ruthie. She looked a bit sleep-groggy, uncombed of hair, and wore nothing except a white tee shirt which came down to her navel. She was staring at him levelly with those eyes-beyond-her-years.

Moon returned the gadget to the dressing gown pocket and cleared his throat. He said, "I'm a biologist. Uh, something like a doctor. I was checking the room to see if there were any germs."

She looked at him, seemingly neither accepting nor rejecting. She said, "There aren't any here. If there was I woulda seen them."

Moon said, "Uh, they're very tiny, little girl."

"I'm not a little girl. I'm going on ten."

"Good point; sorry. What did you want?"

Her eyes narrowed slightly, and had she been even a few years older, he would have thought sleepily sensuous. She said, "I wanted to watchya dress. I never seen anybody your color before. You're kinda pretty."

Moon inwardly winced at that but he said, "Well, I

don't like to have people, particularly little . . . that is, young ladies watch me dress."

"Why?" she said flatly. "You got something wrong with you?" There was interest in her sultry voice.

"No. And now, kindly buzz off."

She shrugged a very adult shrug and turned and obeyed orders.

When she was gone, Bowser said, "Jesus."

Moon closed the door the child had opened silently, and looked down at the knob. There was no way of locking it. Evidently, the Chutzpa family didn't see any need for locks.

Moon went over to his suitcase, discarded the dressing gown, pajama bottoms which he had worn without tops, and slippers, then dressed in the same informal clothing he had worn the day before. Then he left the room, carrying his toothbrush and powder and headed for the community bathroom.

There was no one there, either, so he washed face, hands and teeth, utilizing the provided soap and handmade towels and made his way back to his room. He hadn't wanted to take the time to shower. Franny had driven him somewhat hurriedly about the small soul-farm, as they called it, the day before when they had first arrived, but he wanted the opportunity to look the place over thoroughly before more of the family appeared on the scene.

However, that wasn't to be. When he emerged from the patio, now followed by the shock of hair that was Bowser, this time it was to come upon a smiling Zack.

Zack looked down at the dog and, before addressing the family guest, said, "Good morning, Bowser."

And Bowser said, a trace of yawn in his squeaky voice, "Good morning."

Zack stared down at him unbelievingly, as though he still didn't trust his own senses. Then he looked up at Moon and said, "Good morning. Wasn't the room comfortable?"

Moon said, "Oh, it was fine but I guess I'm thrown off by the changes in the clock out here. I thought I'd take a little stroll and look the place over."

"I'll come along."

"Don't let me bother you."

"No bother. I'll show you the whole shebang. You might miss some things, like Sun Valley." Zack was obviously anxious to be with the other.

Giving up, Moon turned and, the younger man beside him, headed for the stairway that led to the surface.

"Sun Valley?" he said.

"Yeah," Zack told him, looking back over his shoulder to be sure that Bowser was still bringing up the rear and could successfully navigate the stairs with his short legs. "Our solar plant. We've got it tucked away in a kind of little valley where you can't see it until you come up close. It's not particularly attractive."

They had been walking over the almost lawn-like grass. A few yards from the dwelling they'd just left and it was difficult to make out where it was. The family had done a beautiful job of camouflaging with the materials nature had provided.

"Solar plant?" Moon said. "You generate your own power?"

"Sure. Almost all places like this do. The government kind of subsidizes building them, especially in places out here in the boondocks. Saves spending in power lines. We've got about an acre in our solar collector." He looked over his shoulder. "We walking too fast for you, Bowser?"

"Jesus, no," Bowser said. His little red tongue came out through his facial hair and he gave a quick double pant.

Zack gave the newcomer a thorough inspection of the family estate. In Moon's eyes, it was more of a truck gardening project than a farm, though there were orchards of fruit and other trees, rimming it. What they had told him the night before was borne out. They supplemented their necessities, especially their food supply, but were actually dependent upon their Government Annual Stipend.

The whole place was charming enough and more like a park than a farm in the old sense. There were no fences and the artesian well-irrigated area which they had homesteaded fell off into rather desolate prairie, almost semi-desert, as soon as their cultivated area gave out.

Zack said, looking over at the other from the side of his eyes, "Franny had a lot of good things to say about you to Blackie. She thought you'd make a swell addition to the family."

"You're looking for new members?"

"Oh, sure. Always, but especially these days. We had a family council not so long ago and decided to make an effort to enlarge. Additional family members make things more interesting. They've got new ideas, new viewpoints and new skills, for that matter. For instance, I imagine a biologist would be able to help us with the crops, the animals and all."

Moon moistened his lower lip and said slowly, "Then you expect quite a few newcomers, strangers, to be coming around?"

Zack made one of his monkey faces at that. "Well, no. Not real quickly, at least. We're pretty demanding. Pretty selective. If you're not careful, in a family, you wind up with people that cause trouble. For instance, like you were asking last night. What happens if you have a family member who doesn't want to do his share of the work? It's supposed to be we don't give a damn, of course, but the way the family is now everybody does do his share and everybody wants to. Golly, even the Twins get out and help pick vegetables and fruits, when something's ripe. But if you got a half dozen deadbeats on the place, sooner or later it'd probably lead to bad feelings."

"I can see that," Moon said. "I don't like lazies myself but the world as it is is certainly creating a lot of them. Nine people out of ten in this country are on GAS."

Zack shrugged it off. "There's nothing you can do about it, what with automation and computerization and all. Machines do all the work."

Moon looked over at him. They were standing on a small knoll, looking out over a well kept apple orchard. He said, his voice with an exploratory aspect, "Are you so sure there's nothing to be done about it?"

"Why sure. The government wouldn't be paying us all GAS if we could find jobs. There just aren't many jobs."

"Possibly there could be, if some changes were made," Moon said. "The thing is, those who control the socioeconomic system in this country these days are afraid of change. They don't want the applecart upset, the boat rocked. They'd rather see the people on GAS. They'd rather pony up and keep the people docile. The Romans were another example of the same situation. For centuries, they kept the Roman proletariat on free bread and circuses, to keep them quiet. Those on the freebies list, on a pension, or Social Security, or relief by whatever name, are always conservative, Zack. They're scared to death that something will happen to their freeloading privileges. Nobody was quicker to tear down the would-be reformer than the Roman mob. They *wanted* the status quo. When the Gracchi came along,—the Gracchus brothers, Gaius and Tiberius, —recommending basic changes in the Roman system, so that the people would again have land and other opportunities, and a larger say in the running of the republic, it was the proletariat that killed them. No, the people who cause trouble, who want changes in government and institutions are those who are active, alert, interested and involved in things. Don't look for your revolutionists among the pensioners, even when the pension is inadequate. Don't look for demands for change from people on GAS, they don't want change.''

This whole approach was new to Zack. It had never occurred to him. Not even Bitter Joe had ever come up with the equivalent.

He said, complaint in his voice, ''But there are no jobs. Even if we all wanted to work in industry, or wherever, they don't need us.''

The larger man looked at him strangely. ''Are you so sure? Admittedly, a minimum of workers are needed in factories or mines, or on ships or in aircraft, or other means of transportation. Or in distribution or communications, for that matter. But how about the space program? What happened to it?''

''The Department of Scientific Research said it was too expensive.''

''With tens of millions of people out of work and on the dole? Or how about research programs? The human race must not stand still, it's got to continue to advance. Those currently in the catbird seat are afraid of advance and change. Once again, it might upset the applecart. But scientific research isn't the only thing we could be devoting our working lives to, if we were given the chance. How about the arts, how about more advanced education for all? How about putting a few million people to work, and a few billion pseudo-dollars, into ecology and beautifying the country in general? There's one hell of a lot still to be done in such fields, Zack. Your family has beautified this part of the country, these few acres, but as a whole the nation is one big eyesore. The first Pilgrim that landed in New England began the process of making America a garbage dump and it's been going on ever since.''

Zack had no answer to the argument. He said, unhappily, ''Well, let's go back to The Barn. I'll show you how the Doc makes hard cider and then applejack.''

They resumed their stroll. Short-legged Bowser, tip of tongue now hanging out, but game, continued to bring up the rear. Largely he kept his peace, though once he had said, ''Jesus, I could use a drink.''

And Zack had looked back at him and said, ''Golly, I'm sorry. There's nice fresh water at The Barn.''

On the way to the Barn, they passed a pool, a pond covering an area of two acres or so. There were two small boats pulled up upon the shore.

''That's the fish pond,'' Zack said proudly.

Moon asked the polite questions.

The other was a young man of enthusiasms and went into detail upon farming fish. The Doc had come upon the idea whilst browsing through National Data Bank's papers devoted to soul farming. As soon as Sun Valley was producing enough power for the project, they sank a well, located a natural depression on their land that wasn't being utilized, built a bit of dam, and flooded it. They had then imported several thousand largemouth bass fingerlings and several tens of thousands of several varieties of bream and dumped them in. At first they'd had to fertilize the pond but by now it had achieved a balance. The bass ate the bream, which fed on small life and vegetation, and the family had both the sport of catching the bass and the pleasure of eating them. Even the Twins loved fishing and participated by angling for bream with small poles, complete with line and corks, their hooks baited with worms.

"That was a good baked bass we had yesterday," Moon said. "Do you get enough fish to supply all of your wants?"

"Golly, yeah," the younger man assured him. "More than enough. We trade off quite a few bass to another family that raises beef cattle. We don't have steers."

They resumed their way toward the Barn.

Moon said, "I understand that Colleen is the only family member working at a job on the outside."

"Yeah," Zack said. "She's the office worker at the Ultra-Market in Coronado. Ron's been trying to write for a long time but he's never sold any of his stuff. And I've been trying to dream up a good novelty idea, something like a fad, but I haven't come up with anything so far. If I could just hit on a real far-out new idea." He shrugged it off. "Do you think you'll want to come in with us, Moon?"

The other worked that over before saying, "I don't know. Actually, what I really wanted to do, now that my job's gone, was to see the Americas. Travel all the way down through Mexico, through Central America and then down into Peru and that country. There's a great deal to interest a biologist down there, both in the jungles and high mountains. And I'm fascinated by the Inca culture too. I'd like to see the ruins."

Zack said, "Golly, that sounds great. Are you going to do it?"

Moon made a wry face. "I doubt it. A single person on GAS has enough to barely get by, and travel is expensive. I couldn't swing it. Besides, how in the hell would I be able to take Bowser along, traveling in second-class buses and all that sort of thing?"

Zack came to a sudden halt and inspiration came to his face.

Moon stopped too and turned and said, "What's the matter?"

Zack put out a hand and touched the other on the arm. "Listen," he said excitedly. "I told you about my looking for a novelty idea that'd really wow a helluva lot of people. What about breeding talking dogs? The family's got the place here, and we've got the manpower to do it. If we bought ourselves another couple of Sazarac terriers for breeding, in no time flat we'd be turning out talking dogs like crazy."

Moon looked at him as though the other had slipped around the bend.

Zack said urgently, "I mean, you sell Bowser to us."

Moon said indignantly, "Fine, but I wouldn't sell Bowser. We've been friends all his life. I was instrumental in the experiments that . . ."

Zack raised his voice above him. "I'm talking about enough pseudo-dollars to finance that trip of yours all the way through the Americas."

"Don't be silly," Moon snorted. "Holy smokes, you're on GAS yourself. Where'd you get that many credits?"

"The family," Zack said excitedly. "We've been kind of saving to buy a pick-up hover-truck. We need it here on the farm. We don't begin to spend all of our GAS. It accumulates, especially with Colleen kicking in her weekly paychecks.''

The bargaining for Bowser began.

Chapter Seven

John Shay had been impatient during the several days he had spent taking instruction from experts of the Division of Clandestine Services of the Inter-American Bureau of Investigation. Inwardly, he didn't believe any of it necessary. If you had a contract to hit a man, it was simple. You found him, preferably after somebody fingered him for you, and you went about your business. The time he had spent learning about hush-hush methods of communication at the Division's secret station, and the time devoted to off-beat weapons of assassination, had been wasted. For instance, what in the hell use had he for a poison undetectable even if an autopsy was immediately made on the victim?

However, he bore it. If the Director played fair, it was the best assignment John Shay had ever had. It promised an easy life for the balance of his days. And a way out. For nearly a year now he'd had certain apprehensions about the higher-ups who usually employed him. He knew too much. It was the worst business in the world in which to know too much. He suspected that he had been living on borrowed time. He suspected that he still was. He had no guarantee that Director Roy Thomas was not as worried about someone knowing too much as was one of the Syndicate's godfathers. There was no guarantee that after his mission had been accomplished he wouldn't be considered expendable.

And he had no other choice.

He bore his instruction and the mystery atmosphere that had been perpetuated throughout it. He was known only, to the agents who dealt with him, as Mr. Shay. And they made no effort whatsoever to delve further into him. He had been assigned a small suite and all his meals were served there by a waiter who could have been a deaf-mute. He had been offered a selection of potables for after-hours relaxation but had refused them. John Shay did practically no drinking. As a matter of fact, he didn't smoke either and most certainly was on no drug. He even refrained from female companionship save for two or three times a year when he would pick up a fabulously endowed call girl and spend a weekend of concentrated sex with her. He never repeated with the same girl.

But now he was to be interviewed by the Director again. He suspected the reason was to get his final instructions.

The interview was largely a duplication of the first, without the routine of his being frisked for a weapon at the door which led to Roy Thomas' sanctum sanctorium. The same guard with whom he'd had the run-in the first time was posted at the entry and that worthy gave him a cold glance from the side of his eyes but there were no words between them.

John Shay entered the inner office and made his pilgrimage across the full length of the room. This time, a chair was waiting. Without invitation, he took it and looked at the bureaucrat across the wide expanse of desk. It was the other's ball; let him start bouncing it.

Roy Thomas grumbled heavily, "So: we now get down to the nitty-gritty. You are fully prepared to take on your assignment?"

"That's right," Shay said, between his thin lips. "I was ready four days ago."

"Very well." The older man leaned back in his big swivel chair. He took in the professional killer for a long heavy moment as though not quite sure how to begin. Finally, he said, "Mr . . . ah, Shay, do you consider yourself to be a patriotic American?"

Shay looked at him expressionlessly, wordlessly.

Thomas made a grunting sound in his chest. He said, "If you follow the news at all, you are acquainted with the fact that one of the most momentous periods of this nation's history is being gone through. Representatives of all political elements—I might say, save one—are gathered in a Second Constitutional Convention whose purpose is to draw up a Revised Constitution."

"I heard about it," Shay said, then added. "But I thought all the parties were there. Even the smallest ones."

"In a way. Each political party is represented proportionally. Even the smallest have one delegate. The Democratic-Republicans, of course, have hundreds."

"What's this one that isn't there?"

"That's what I was coming to. They refuse to show themselves. The old term was, they've gone underground."

John Shay was out of his depth and had learned long since to clam up under such a situation.

The Director seemed to take another tack. He said slowly, "Mr. Shay, have you ever heard of Thomas Paine?"

"No."

"He's the man most responsible for the American Revolution, or at least, for its developing to the point where the colonists declared their independence."

"I thought it was George Washington."

"No. Washington and Benjamin Franklin, and some of the others usually called our Revolutionary Forefathers, got on the bandwagon rather late in the game. Paine was the pamphleteer who actually precipitated complete revolt, and then, as the war progressed, kept it going with his series of pamphlets entitled *The Crisis*."

"All right. What in the hell's all this got to do with me?"

Roy Thomas took him in for a long moment before saying, "Mr. Shay, suppose that the British had sent in a hit man six months before Thomas Paine wrote his booklet *Common Sense*?"

John Shay replied with a silent shrug. It was Thomas' top, let him spin it.

The Director went on. "You've heard of Karl Marx and Friedrich Engels?"

"The first one was that big Communist, wasn't he? A Russian, or something."

"Marx and Engels were the founders of so-called Scientific Socialism, as opposed to Utopian Socialism which preceded it. They were active in Europe, especially France and Germany, when still youths. They wrote the *Communist Manifesto* there. By the way, don't confuse them with the pseudo-Communists in the Soviet Complex and China, who call themselves Communists and pay lip service to Marx and Engels, but that's about all. Their politico-economic system is best described as State Capitalism. At any rate, the revolution they sponsored in 1848 failed. They fled to England where Marx was allowed political refuge and spent the rest of his life working on analyzing the capitalist system, and predicting its ultimate overthrow. Actually, he was a scholar, rather than what we usually think of as a revolutionist.''

John Shay wasn't noted for his attention span and now he was getting bored. ''What's this got to do with me?'' he said again.

Roy Thomas nodded his bulldog head. ''Very well. Suppose the British government, instead of granting refuge, had imprisoned Karl Marx rather than letting him spend the rest of his life in the British Museum researching *Das Kapital*?''

Shay said impatiently, ''If I'm guessing what you're leading up to: you wanta find some guy who's like this Paine and Karl Marx, before he does his dirty work.''

Roy Thomas wasn't capable of beaming but he did his equivalent. However, Shay spoke again before the Director was able to congratulate him.

John Shay said, ''It's a lot of crap. You don't know what a guy's going to write until he writes it. The British couldn't have hit this guy Paine and they couldn't have tossed this Karl Marx into the slammer, because they didn't know they were dangerous, ahead of time.''

And the other nodded agreement. ''Quite right. They couldn't have done it *then*. But that was before the day of the computer and the National Data Banks.''

John Shay blinked usually expressionless eyes at him.

And now Roy Thomas came to the point. ''I told you that we didn't know his name. That's not quite correct. His name is Ross Prager but he changes it . . . often. He's on the run. His whole organization, the so-called Posterity Party, is underground. We can round them up, periodically, and we do. But largely they're not important and there's not much we can hold them for. There are too many to jail them all, even with trumped-up evidence, and most of them are unimportant anyway.''

"Now, wait a minute," Shay protested. "What'd ya mean he's gone on the run? That doesn't make sense. He's got to have his Universal Credit Card. He's got to have pseudo-dollars to his credit in the National Data Banks Banking Section. You can't go in a restaurant, or a hotel. Christ, you can't do anything without a credit card. Take a taxi, get groceries or a pair of socks in an ultra-market . . . anything. You've got to have a credit card. And if he uses his, you've got him.''

Thomas sighed heavily. "Usually, he doesn't have one at all. Sometimes he does. And he gets it the same way you got your papers—illegally, which means they don't hold up indefinitely. But he's continually changing identification. Some of the Posterity Party members work in key jobs in the National Data Banks and they stick their necks out. Goddamned martyrs. We nail them, eventually, of course, but meanwhile, Ross Prager keeps on the run.''

"But he's got to eat! He's got to have a credit card he's using, and, like you say, it doesn't take you long to track down the best fakes possible.''

Thomas sighed from deep down in his hefty belly. "He has at least one, sometimes two, sometimes more, Party members running front man for him.''

"Front man?''

The Director explained. "In the early days of this Bureau we were largely employed in hunting down bank robbers, kidnappers, that sort of thing. Johnny Dillinger,

Bonnie and Clyde, Baby Face Nelson, Pretty Boy Floyd, Alvin Karpis, Ma Barker and her boys. You've probably never heard of any of them.''

"I heard of Bonnie and Clyde. One of those rerun movies once.''

Thomas inwardly flinched but he said, "Very well. They invariably were too hot to reveal themselves, so they had one or more front men, or whatever term you want to use. It wouldn't do for Public Enemy Number One, whose face was in every post office, to show himself. When he wanted to put up for the night, he'd send his front man, actually often a woman, ahead to rent a room, to buy food or booze, ammunition, or anything else he couldn't afford to be seen doing. Bonnie did it for Clyde Barrow, and Baby Face Nelson's wife did it for him. Then, after the motel, or whatever, was rented, the big shot Public Enemy would quietly move in at night. Nobody knew he was in the vicinity until he pulled the caper on the local bank, or whatever.''

"That's the way this Prager guy operates?''

"More or less. Even if he currently has a forged Universal Credit Card, he seldom if ever uses it. His front man, or woman, handles all that. He keeps on the move.''

"Hell,'' Shay said in disgust. "With all the resources you people are supposed to have, all you got to do is run down the front man. Then you've got Prager.''

"They keep changing them. When we catch one, possibly months afterwards, we have nothing on him. He's done nothing illegal. All he's done is buy Prager meals, hotel rooms, clothes and so forth.''

"But for a fugitive. Sheltering a fugitive, isn't that illegal?''

"He's not a fugitive.''

Shay was staring again. "Damn it, you just said that he was on the run."

"Yes, but we have no charges against him. He's doing it on his own. He knows that we'll nail him if he stands still, on some trumped-up charge. But it's all . . . under the hat. In actuality, he's broken no laws."

"All right, damn it," the professional assassin said in irritation. "Let's go back a ways. Why don't you grab one of these front guys you were talking about and twist his arm a little, with Scop or some other truth serum or whatever, and find out where the bastard is?"

"Because they don't know. As soon as they leave the job of running interference for him, somebody else takes over and the old one doesn't know Prager's future plans. They're not informed by the Posterity Party National Executive Committee."

"Blue jazus. I swear, the more I talk to you about this screwed-up deal the less I know. I still don't know why this Prager character is so dangerous."

The Director growled, "The country is in a state of flux. With the Second Constitutional Convention in session, a good many of the people are thinking in terms of change. Some of them in terms of fundamental change. All we need is a spark and we might have millions in revolt against our Ultra-Welfare State, or People's Capitalism, as some call it. Thus far, Prager has written three pamphlets. The first was a comparatively mild call for socioeconomic reforms. Then he evidently came in contact with the Posterity Party."

"What in the hell's that?"

"Briefly, they contend that the country ought to start thinking of the future, planning ahead as to what we want to accomplish for ourselves and posterity. And the more they do such planning, the greater the changes they advocate. They claim that our present society is an *Apres nous le deluge* socioeconomic system.''

''A what?'' Shay scowled.

''It's a quotation from Madame de Pompadour,'' the Director explained patiently. ''She was the mistress of Louis Fifteenth of France. It means, *After us the deluge.*''

''I still don't get it.''

Thomas said, less patiently now, ''The aristocracy of France was living high on the hog, but at the price of the future. The Posterity Party says that we've got to begin planning with the following generations in mind. That we can't keep fouling up the ecology, wasting our raw materials, leaving idle nine-tenths of the working force. By the way: ''After Us, The Deluge'' is the title of one of Prager's pamphlets.

''All right, go on,'' Shay said. ''They sound like a bunch of fruitcakes. The country's never had it so good. Everybody eats, everybody's got a home, at least of sorts. Those who can't get a job have Tri-Di to watch.''

''Exactly,'' the Director nodded. ''So Prager came in contact with the Posterity Party and became more radical. He also became the party theoretician and the rest of them soon realized that he was their intellectual leader, and began to protect him. Membership grew, faster than we were able to do anything about it. His second and third pamphlets went considerably further than his first. It's to be assumed that he is now working on a fourth, and, frankly, with the country all taken up with the new proposed Revised Constitution, we don't want to see it hit print.''

Shay eyed him questioningly. ''Why not just suppress it?''

"No. Impossible. We can drag our heels on publicizing it, we can give it the silent treatment, no reviews, so that word of mouth is the only way the people will get to know about it, but tell the American people that they can't read something and it's the surest way of guaranteeing they will, even if it has to be secretly duplicated in cellars. Prager is good at what he does in print media; you could call him a medium out of control."

"Out of *your* control, you mean," Shay said wryly. "But how do you know this next thing he writes is going to be a blockbuster?"

"The computers say so. They say he's the greatest potential danger to our present socioeconomic system. And if his message spreads, the Posterity Party will be in a position to put over its program in three and a half years, give or take six months."

Shay said, disbelief in his voice, "I never even heard of them. How could they take over the works in three and a half years?"

The bureaucrat stretched out a hand toward one of the desk drawers and it automatically opened. He brought forth a paper and stared unhappily at it.

"This is from Lenin, the leading figure of the Russian Revolution. He didn't foresee when or in what form his revolution would erupt until it was almost on him. This is what he said in January 1917, one month before the February Revolution and only ten months before the October Revolution which brought him to power. He was talking to a gathering of Swiss Socialists."

Roy Thomas read: "*We the older generation, perhaps will not live to see the . . . approaching revolution. But, I can, it seems to me, express with extreme confidence the hope that the youth . . . of the whole world will have the good fortune to emerge victorious in the approaching revolution of the proletariat.''*

He sighed and put the paper down. ''The same thing applied in the American Revolution. The colonists were up in arms, but all they wanted was relief from taxes and more say in their own government. It never occurred to them to fight for full independence. But then Paine wrote *Common Sense* in January of 1776 and six months later the Declaration of Independence was signed. No, given the material conditions and a medium out of control, a revolutionary change can take place practically overnight.''

Shay was getting tired of it all. ''Okay,'' he said. ''So what are my instructions?''

''You locate and eliminate Prager, making it seem an accident if possible.''

''You pony up the expenses for all this?''

The Director shook his head. ''Finance it yourself. We want no records in the data banks showing that you have any connections with us. It's the main reason we're using your services rather than one of our people.''

Shay took a deep breath. ''How do I find this Ross Prager?''

''You'll carry a tightbeam communicator. When he's flushed, we'll let you know. Our leads indicate his present front might be a certain Francesca de Rudder . . .''

''Francesca de Rudder!'' Shay blurted.

''Yes, the well-publicized rocket-set member of the de Rudder family. She's a mad-cap and why she wants a change in the country, God only knows. We suspect she's a member of the Posterity Party. The last time she used her Universal Credit Card was to make payment for a recharging of her power packs for her hover-car in a small town called Coronado in New Mexico. That's where you're headed.''

For a moment, the bulldog face of the Director seemed to sag in weariness. He said, and the tiredness was in his voice as well, ''Mr. Shay, perhaps you do not concern yourself with patriotism. However, the social system of your country is at stake and you confront the most dangerous man in our nation.''

Shay misunderstood momentarily, and his eyes narrowed when he said, ''He goes heeled?''

''No, not in the way you mean. But in the most dangerous way, emphatically yes. He writes.''

Chapter Eight

The family made a practice of each member making his or her own breakfast whenever the spirit moved. The only exceptions were the Twins. When they appeared on the morning scene, whatever adult was present took their breakfast orders—within reason. Dietary rules were slack in the family, but the two gremlins weren't allowed ice cream and cookies for their first meal, though they were working on the project.

The kitchen was roomy, in the old farm kitchen tradition of early America, and had a table up against one wall that could accommodate ten or twelve persons at a time, on the few occasions when that many showed up at once. It was warm with friendly odors and had every kitchen device, save anything mechanical. In fact, the most mechanical device boasted was a hand-operated eggbeater and it was seldom used. The Doc, in particular, railed that eggs should be whomped up with loving care using a silver fork.

Blackie was busy at the stove when the Wizard entered. The Twins were banging away on the table with knives and forks. The honey jar had been moved carefully away by the family elder, for preservation against both appetite and mayhem.

When the bespectacled one-man brain trust of the family entered, Blackie said, "I'm doing scrambled eggs for myself and the twins, dear, would you like some?"

"I'd like French toast," the Wizard said, putting a note pad and pencil he'd been carrying down on the table and taking a stool.

"Then you'll sure as hell make your own."

"We'll have French toast too," one of the Twins shrilled, knowing cinnamon and sugar could be amply sprinkled on this dish.

"Shut up, dear," Blackie said, going on with tucking the eggs in and about a copper frying pan with a spatula.

She said to the Wizard, "You're usually the first one to breakfast, sweetie, what spins?"

"I've been listening to the news."

"On an empty stomach? Must've been juicy."

"The Mafia Party thinks that the government should be handed over to them. You know, at the Second Constitutional Convention."

"Mafia?" the family elder said placidly, "When I was a girl, the Mafia . . ."

"Times have changed," the Wizard told her with his usual insufferable superiority. "They claim they're all legal now. Very legal. But they've still got their organization and say that they work more efficiently than the present government. So they're willing to take over . . . for a small percentage."

Blackie began rattling dishes around, preparatory to serving up the eggs. "What else?" she said, not particularly caring. Like Bitter Joe, she was largely allergic to the news.

"The Marijuanero Apaches. According to one unconfirmed dispatch, they've ripped off over a ton of plastique explosives from a Federal armory up near Colorado Springs."

Blackie said vaguely, "Oh? How nice. What in the hell are they going to do with it?"

"The dispatch says Buffalo Dong claims that they're going to blow up the Hoover Dam, and wash half of Baja California into the ocean."

"Holy hell," she said, eyes slightly wider. "Who did you say they were?"

"The Marijuanero Apaches. They've gone on the warpath. The reservation was surrounded by the National Guard, State Police, elements of the Air Force and a lot of vigilantes, but when they closed in, the whole of Geronimo County—that's their reservation—was found abandoned. Towns and all. Not a single soul." The Wizard added with satisfaction, "They've undoubtedly headed for the hills. The leader of the vigilantes says that not a man, woman or child in the southwest is safe. He's president of United Uranium. He wants them all shot on sight."

"Who, dear?" Blackie said, putting the eggs, along with home-cured bacon and country biscuits, in front of the twins. The twins immediately grabbed for the apple jelly jar.

The Wizard said patiently, "Gerald Fouler. The newsmen call him Jerk Fouler. He says the government ought to confiscate the reservation and turn its uranium over to private enterprise and move the Marijuaneros onto a smaller reservation, possibly in Death Valley over in California.

How that jibes with shooting them all on sight, I don't know.''

"I'll be damned. It certainly sounds terrible, dear. Nobody has been hurt, have they?''

"Not exactly,'' the Wizard told her condescendingly. "They haven't been able to find Buffalo Dong and his braves. But the Air Force helio-jets dropped a whole lot of some new gas they've got—it was the first chance they had to try it—on a lot of vigilante militia and State Police by mistake. The stuff makes you toss your cookies and cry for about a week.''

Blackie took her own place at the table, next to the twins, and absentmindedly pushed the jelly jar to one side. Too late. They'd both managed to dollop out a quarter pound or so each onto their plates and were wading into the biscuits, as eggs and bacon went cold.

"Hell,'' Blackie said. "The things that happen. You go ahead and make your French toast, Wizard. How did you do in your chess game the other night?''

"I played Bitter Joe, Zack, the Professor, the Doc, Colleen and Ron, all at once. And I was blindfolded.''

"I'll be damned. How did you make out?''

"I lost all six games.'' He went back to his war communique. "One reporter dug out the fact that over the past few months three antiaircraft guns, war relics that were out on the front lawns of city halls in several towns not too far from Geronimo County, have been ripped off.''

"What's an antiaircraft gun, dear? And who in the hell'd want to steal one?''

"They're for shooting down airplanes. The reporter says that Buffalo Dong's braves got them and have probably repaired them. The commander of the National Guard,

General Peckerflogger, wants all airline flights over New Mexico canceled.''

"Peckerflogger? That can't be his name, dear.''

"It's something like that,'' the Wizard said, getting up and beginning to accumulate the ingredients for his French toast.

JoJo, yawning prettily, barefooted and attired only in a diaphanous nightgown, came in.

JoJo looked like this: She was Black Irish. She was Southern Italian. She was the Jewess, Rebecca, in *Ivanhoe*. She had long, luxurious, infinitely soft, jet black hair and her complexion was the peaches and cream you're always reading about but practically never see. Her generous mouth had no need whatsoever for lipstick, and had it not been for her youth her unbelievably perfect teeth would have been suspect as the product of a show-off dentist. And her face did not detract from her figure. She looked like Elizabeth Taylor, a few years after the actress had played in *National Velvet*.

Blackie said, "Good morning, dear. I'm afraid that the twins and I have taken all of the goddamned eggs I just cooked. But the Wizard is doing French toast.''

JoJo yawned winningly and said, "All I want is coffee, right now.''

"Where is everybody?'' the Wizard said.

"They're out in the patio saying goodbye to Moon.''

Blackie said, in matronly distress, "Goodbye? You mean he's leaving? Holy hell, Franny was so sure that he'd like it here and would want to join the family.''

"That's too bad,'' the Wizard said, halting his dipping of slices of bread into egg batter. "I wanted to talk to him more about how he altered the genes of that dog. I was wondering if it'd be possible to raise frogs with four hind legs, out in the fish pond. Let's go and see if we can't coax him into staying.''

Blackie came to her feet. "Oh, crap," she said. "Franny will be upset. I do hope he didn't consider us inhospitable. Perhaps the boys gave him too much of the Doc's apple-jack and made him puke. They were kind of knocking it back before we all went to bed.''

JoJo said, ''I don't think it was that. I heard him say something to the effect that he never got so drunk that he couldn't urinate.''

The Wizard looked at her, sorrow behind his glasses, but he said, ''Maybe he was lonesome. How come one or two of you girls didn't sleep with him?''

They trooped toward the patio, leaving the twins behind, and that brace of unlikely cherubs immediately snagged the jelly jar again.

Moon's bag was all packed and sitting on the flagstones of the patio while he went about shaking hands with the gathered family, all of whom looked sad to see him going, save Zack, who had a pleased-as-punch smirk on his ugly phiz.

When the big man had made his goodbyes and had listened to the various protests of his leaving, he wound up by saying, ''It's not that I don't like you all, and like the place. It's fine; justifies everything Franny told me about it. By the way, tell her goodbye for me. Sorry I missed her. But I've had this ambition to see Latin America for years and can't give it up.''

He looked down at Bowser who was sitting to one side, in the shade of a lilac bush. ''So long, old buddy,'' he said sadly.

Bowser looked up at him. ''You sonofabitch,'' he said. ''After all we've meant to each other. Here you go selling me to this orangutan-faced slob, who wants to turn me into a full-time stud, just because I can talk.''

All eyes went first to Bowser, then to Zack who, on the face of it, was the only one of the group who fitted that description.

Ron blurted, ''Sell you!''

Moon looked miserable.

Bowser said, disgust in his somewhat squeaky voice, ''Well, all I can say is, I may be a talking dog, but I'll never say another word in my life.''

Moon shook his head in sorrow, but reached down and took up his bag and started up the stairs to the surface.

Rusty looked at the suddenly distressed Zack. ''Christ,'' she said. ''What's going on here?''

But Zack was staring down at the dog. ''Golly, you don't mean that!'' he blurted.

Bowser put out his little red tongue from amidst all the hair and gave a double pant.

The Doc echoed Rusty's demand. ''What's going on here?'' he said.

''I bought Bowser,'' Zack said, his tone on the defiant side.

They were all staring at him now, all who weren't staring at the shock of dirty black hair that was the dog.

''Bought Bowser?'' Bitter Joe said blankly.

''Yeah, yeah,'' Zack said in earnest explanation. ''It hit me like a ton of bricks.''

''Good grief, I'm beginning to suspect it's going to hit the rest of us like a ton of shit,'' the Professor muttered.

Zack hurried on, his voice plaintive. ''Don't you see? It's the thing I've been talking about for so long. A novelty idea that'll wow the whole country. A fad that'll take on like crazy. Talking dogs. You heard what Moon said last night, and he's a biologist. All we have to do is breed Bowser to a bitch Sazarac and right from the beginning half of the litter will be able to talk. Then we keep breeding back and in no time at all, we'll be breeding true. All the pups will be smart—able to talk. They'll sell like hotcakes. Don't you see? We've got it made.''

Sweet Alice, looking as prettily blank as usual, contemplated Bowser. ''He said he wouldn't talk anymore,'' she said. ''He's mad at Moon. He probably won't even screw any females.''

Bowser looked up at her and his hairy rear end showed faint signs of stirring. It was the nearest thing he could accomplish in the way of wagging.

Blackie said to Zack, sudden suspicion in her voice, ''Dear, what in the name of hell did you pay for him?''

Zack swallowed and looked at her apprehensively.

Ron said, ''Yeah. What'd you pay for him?''

And now the whole family was eyeing the unhappy Zack accusingly, even little Ruthie who had never bought anything in her life, never having had occasion to.

Zack swallowed again and said, his voice pleading, ''Everything.''

Bitter Joe said ominously, ''What d'ya mean, everything?''

''Everything we had in the family account.''

Most of them were speechless at that, but Rusty got out, ''Christ, you mean all the pseudo-dollars we've saved toward the hover-truck?''

The Professor said, ''Good lord, you can't mean all the family savings, too. The emergency fund and our basic nest egg, in case we want to buy more land or construct new buildings.''

Zack looked at him dumbly.

"Jeepers," little Ruthie said. She looked down at Bowser, whose red tongue was out again. "All for a pooch no bigger than that?"

Zack put his hands out in supplication and said desperately to the others, "But don't you see? He's a thoroughbred Sazarac and a talking dog."

Sweet Alice was still taking Bowser in, her expression characteristically shining. "But he said he wouldn't talk anymore."

Zack groaned. "He was just kidding. He was just sore. Weren't you, Bowser?"

Bowser looked up at him, on hearing his name, but held his peace.

Zack groaned again.

Franny, frowning puzzlement, and looking back over her shoulder, came down the steps leading from the surface into the patio of the underground building.

She said, "That couldn't have been Moon I just saw going down the road?"

Franny looked like this: Somewhere in her early thirties, she had a certain flair. Her face was fresh and bright, though by no means with the same low-wattage brightness as that of Sweet Alice. She was well-dressed, by family standards, in sports clothes, and her posture was excellent, that of an accomplished horsewoman. She was darkish blonde, a little too thin, and tall. She looked like Candice Bergen playing some part which involved considerable earnestness.

"Yeah," Bitter Joe said bitterly. "With the family fortune, such as it is, transferred to his credit account."

Franny scowled at him. "What in the world are you

talking about? I was hoping he'd like it here. That he'd become a member of the family.''

Zack hoped he might gain an adherent. "He sold us . . ."

"He sold *you*," Rusty muttered, shaking her head until her thin ponytail fluttered.

". . . his Sazarac terrier," Zack said. "A talking . . ."

"Sazarac?" Franny said indignantly. "That's a cocktail they make over in New Orleans." She looked down at the little dog. "Hello, Bowser," she said.

All of the family looked down as well, hopefully. Bowser wagged his hairy rump at Franny but remained silent.

Zack said, "He told us all about it. A talking dog he, uh, altered when he was a biologist. You know, a scientist. I figured . . ."

"Talking dog?" Franny snorted. "You mean the bastard pulled that old trick on you? He's not much more of a biologist than I am. Maybe a year or two in college."

They all looked at her blankly.

Franny said, "He's a ventriloquist. It's his hobby. He pulled the same trick back when I first met him in New England. Picked up a moth-eaten pup that had a lot of hair on its face, like a sheep dog, so that you couldn't make out his mouth so well, and then peddled it to some cloddy. I'll admit, in that case, what he was really after was a good home for the mutt."

"Ventriloquist?" Zack said, his ugly face not gaining in beauty as misery spread over it.

"That's right," Franny told him. "He's a whiz at it. Besides, he's got some special ventriloquist electronic gizmo he bought in a magic shop, one of those places where magicians buy their props."

Zack closed his eyes in sickness. He said in meaningless misery, "He talked real good."

Franny said, "*Damn* it! He's not going to get away with it. I brought him all the way down here, to join my family, and I'm responsible!"

She turned and started up the stone stairs to the surface, taking them two at a time.

Chapter Nine

Buffalo Dong, better known among his people as Eskininizin, stood on a high outcropping of rock, flanked by three of his followers. Under his arm was a Tokarev MKB 85 (L) laser assault rifle. From this vantage point, he could see a full six miles of highway, as it disappeared to the north into the wasteland. He turned his keen, hard eyes to the left and traced the road in the opposite direction another five miles or more. There were no vehicles to be spotted.

He took off his glasses and slipped them into a shirt pocket and turned to the others.

Buffalo Dong looked like this: Somewhere in his fifties, neither his face nor figure gave indication of his years. He was short and wiry, in the Apache tradition. The black, wire-like hair which covered his head was worn long, bound by a rawhide thong about his head. His face was mahogany, his eyes obsidian, his teeth strong, though somewhat crooked behind thin, dry lips. And at the moment he was wearing war paint. He was dressed in heavy denims, and had slung over his shoulder a leather 'possibles' pouch, worn like the shoulder pocketbooks of women a half century before.

He turned to Marcia Kintpuash, who stood next to him, also taking in the road. She alone of the four wore no facial paint, carried no laser rifle, but there was a sidearm strapped to her right hip.

Buffalo Dong said, in his heavy guttural voice, "What do you think, Marcy?"

She said, "Philosophically speaking, life is but a drooping cigarette between the cynical lips of time."

He looked at her without joy. "Yesterday, you said life was a cigar butt floating down the gutter toward the bottomless sewer of eternity."

Marcy said, "Same thing. You've got to have more than one way of stating your philosophy."

Marcia Kintpuash looked like this: She was a trained nurse and somehow projected the fact despite her attire, which was similar to that of the three Apache men, except that she wore a divided corduroy skirt rather than denim pants. Her dark hair was cut short, rather than worn long like that of the men, but her eyes were Apache black and her figure, though small, was slender and lithe by southwestern Indian standards. Her complexion and pert features indicated that somewhere in the background was other than native blood. She looked quite a bit like Lena Horne at the age of thirty.

Buffalo Dong said, "Okay, but aside from what you think philosophically, what do you think about an ambush here?"

She looked down at the highway again and then at the

road immediately below them where the parked hover-car stood. To both sides of the road were stands of aspens and other mountain trees.

She said, "It looks all right to me."

Buffalo Dong looked over at the other two, both of them standing stoically, both of them hard of body, strong-looking young men in their twenties. Both could have put aside the denims and hiking shoes which duplicated those of their chief, donned feather headdresses and breechcloths and moccasins and gotten jobs as extras massacring Custer in a New Hollywood epic.

He said, "What do you think, boys?"

Jim Aravaipa shrugged and said, "Let's go."

The four started over the rocks and gravel, sliding and slipping down from their perch on the rocks. When they reached the vicinity of the car, the three men faded into the woods while the girl went over to the vehicle and took her place behind the wheel.

She checked the ownership, flicked on the phone and said, "Highway patrol, Highway Patrol. This is Ann Sommerlott. License 1414-69. I have broken down on the road between Arroyo Seco and New View. Could you please get a fix on me and come to my assistance?"

The phone squawked in response. "We'll be there in minutes, Ms."

"Thank you," she said sweetly and switched off.

She slid out of the nurse's kit which was slung over her shoulder and put it on the seat beside her, to ensure being unencumbered, and waited.

Far down the road, she could see the police patrol car coming. She looked back in the other direction. There were no vehicles in sight. They hadn't expected any.

Buffalo Dong had chosen one of the least-travelled highways in the state. Marcy looked up into the sky. She didn't anticipate spotting any aircraft.

The speedy red police car zipped up and parked across the road from her and two uniformed officers issued forth. They looked at her for a narrow-eyed moment and then approached, their gun holsters unbuttoned.

One of them called, "All right, lady. Get out. This car is reported stolen."

Marcy emerged and said easily, "I know. I stole it."

They took her in, especially the holster at her hip. They also took in her appearance.

"An Indian!" one of them blurted.

Their hands started for their guns.

"Ugh, all right, white men," a hidden voice called. "That'll be all. You're covered. Put um up the hands."

The two State Troopers froze; red dots of light, the aim points of laser gun sights, danced on their bodies. Slowly their arms went up.

Buffalo Dong and two of his men stepped out of the woods. All three had their laser assault rifles nonchalantly at ready positions. They walked forward, easily confident.

When they came to a halt, some ten feet off, the eyes of both of the troopers narrowed as they looked at the heavy rifles.

Buffalo Dong said easily, "Ugh. Don't try it, white men. You're covered by more than fifty warriors, including two machine gun teams. Aravaipa, get their guns."

One of the troopers blurted inanely, "You can't do this."

Buffalo Dong looked at him with all the affection of a rattlesnake in heat that has been disturbed from the contemplation of its lady love. He said, "Ugh. You two combatant prisoners of war. We have heard broadcasts. The governor has sent in the State Police after us, along with the National Guard.'' He added, his Indian face expressionless, "Ugh. All you need give is your name, rank and serial number. We Marijuaneros are abiding by the rules of war as set down by the Geneva Convention.''

The lips of the troopers were dry, their faces wan. They didn't believe him. They were both native sons. Both had grandparents who told tales of the days of Geronimo. Both attempted to swallow.

"Ugh. Me Buffalo Dong, War Chief of the Marijuanero Apache Nation,'' the Indian went on. "The Tribal Council has declared that a state of belligerency exists between the Marijuanero Nation and the United States of the Americas.''

They gaped at him.

Jim Aravaipa had lifted their revolvers and stuck them into his own belt. He leered at the two troopers, one of whom repressed a groan. He had seen rerun movies of Dracula getting out of his coffin that looked more reassuring than this painted Apache.

Buffalo Dong said, "Ugh. You have tape unit in your patrol car?''

"Yeah, of course,'' the older of the two managed to say.

The self-announced war chief went over to the red police vehicle, fished around in the dash compartment, and came up with a portable tape machine.

He held it to his mouth, flicked the activating stud and said into it: *"The Marijuanero Apache Tribal Council herewith declares war upon the United States of the Americas and will remain in the field until victorious or until the last warrior has been slain and our last women and children have gone down to the lust of the white men aggressors.''*

At the mention of the lust of the white man, the younger of the troopers gulped and looked over at Marcy Kintpuash who was leaning nonchalantly on the side of the stolen car. She sneered at him. "My great-grandmother was raped at Apache Wells," she said. "We know *your* type."

The trooper gulped again. His grandfather had told him of the old tradition. If in danger of being captured by Apaches, old-timers tried to commit suicide before being turned over to the mercies of the squaws.

Buffalo Dong went on with his taping: "*Less than two centuries ago the Apache people and their cousins the Navahos owned the greater part of the area now known as New Mexico and Arizona. Piece by piece the land was torn from them, cheated away from them. Tribe by tribe, they were defeated by the onslaught of the white aggressors. The great chiefs—Mangas Colorado, Cochise, Victorio, Delshay, Geronimo—were killed in battle, murdered, or imprisoned. Their tribes, the Chiricahua, the Coyoteros, the Jicarillas and the Mescaleros went down to all but oblivion, the young braves killed, the old and weak, the women and children, herded into wasteland that the conquerors were pleased to call reservations. If in time the reservations were found to contain minerals or other valuable raw materials, the Apaches would again be uprooted and herded elsewhere.*"

There came a change in his tone. "*Now we of the Marijuanero Apache nation revolt against the oppression. We issue the following ultimatum, the minimum requirements for peace. So-called Geronimo County shall be a sovereign nation, without interference from the officials of the United States of the Americas. Only our tribal laws will apply. The products of the tribal area shall be the sole property of the Marijuanero Apaches who will be free to market such products, including uranium, on the world market.*

"Until such a peace is signed, we shall fight in the mountains, we shall fight in the forests, we shall fight on the deserts. We shall fight on by all means at our command until victorious, or until we go down to black death. The Marijuanero Apaches call upon all free men of good will throughout the world to rally to our just cause."

He flicked the stud of the tape unit and brought forth the cassette upon which he had been recording, and handed it to the older of the two troopers, both of whom had been staring at him with slack jaws.

"My Gawd," the older trooper muttered to his companion, "this guy is out of control."

Buffalo Dong said, "Ugh. All right. This makes it official. Hand this over to your nearest superior with our instructions that it go first to the governor of the state, and ultimately to the President and Congress of the United States of the Americas. You might pass on the word that it would be of no use to attempt to suppress it. We are sending out copies to the news media and to every member of the Reunited Nations. Our delegation to the Reunited Nations also, obviously, has copies."

"Delegation to the Reunited Nations?" the younger trooper said blankly.

"Ugh. You heard the chief," Jim Aravaipa said.

The older of the two State Police had relief in his voice. He said, "You mean that you're going to turn us loose, to deliver this?"

"Ugh," Buffalo Dong said. "In a manner of speaking. Jim, Hank, bring um into the woods."

He led the way, followed by the two troopers, with the two young Indian warriors bringing up the rear.

In the shelter of the trees, he had them sit down, back to back, and had Jim and Hank appropriate their handcuffs and cuff them together, still back to back, sitting on the ground.

Buffalo Dong said sourly, "Ugh. Okay, Jim. Scalp 'em."

"What!" one of the prisoners ejaculated. "You can't do that!"

Jim leered at him and brought forth from his possibles pouch a battery-powered electric razor and promptly began shaving the tops of the heads of the two policemen until they looked like ordained friars.

Marcy had come up from behind and now shook her head at the sight. "Holy mackerel," she said. "Scalped. That'll get a world-wide horse laugh."

Buffalo Dong said to the prisoners, "Ugh. We're going to leave your car. It won't take too long before somebody back at where ever you have your headquarters gets to worrying about you. When you don't answer your phone, they'll send somebody out. Meanwhile, we're fading off the scene."

"They'll get you!" one of them blurted, trying to drag bravado up from the depths.

"Sure, sure," Jim said. "And when they do—"

"Ugh," Buffalo Dong supplied.

"Right. Ugh," said Jim.

"Let's get out of here," Buffalo Dong ordered, turning and heading for the road.

Marcy looked down at the two disgruntled troopers before following the men. "Ugh, always remember," she told them earnestly. "Existence is but a button passing through the buttonholes of fate in the endless longjohns of time."

"Ugh," said the troopers in unison.

Chapter Ten

By the time Franny returned with the chastened Moon, the day was well along, the noon meal well passed and the family was sitting around glumly save for the twins who were bedeviling Bowser, a fate reserved down through the ages for man's best friend at the hands of man's best children.

The two entered the saloon, Franny all but leading the repentant-looking miscreant by his ear.

While the family looked up at them in disbelief, Franny said, "Tell them you're sorry."

"Fine. I'm sorry."

"Apologize."

"I just did." Moon made a gesture of supplication. "Holy smokes, it was just that he was such a mark that I couldn't resist. I could have sold him the toll privileges for the Brooklyn Bridge."

Rusty looked at Zack, whose expression was almost as

chastened as that of the one who had taken him. She snorted.

Franny said, "He's transferred the full amount back to the family account."

"Ummm," Doc said. "How about a drink, Moon? I've just dug up a barrel of applejack I've been aging for two years. It'll knock you on your butt."

Moon looked relieved at their acceptance of him. "I could use it," he said.

Bowser looked up from where the twins were pulling his inadequate ears and said, "Hi, Boss. Jesus, we sure foxed them, didn't we?"

Moon glared at him indignantly. "You nearly muffed it, you mongrel."

Everybody laughed and what little tension there was disappeared. Doc got half a tumbler of the applejack and handed it over to Moon, who sank apologetically onto a couch next to Franny, as though hoping for continuing support from her.

He said to Zack, "Sorry I bollixed up your big idea for a novelty fad."

"Golly, that's all right," Zack said grudgingly. And then with a return of characteristic optimism, "Sooner or later, I'll think of something else."

"Yeah," Ron said in disgust. "How about a His and Hers Masturbation Kit, for lazy lovers?"

For a moment, Zack actually looked at him with hope.

Three or four of the adults got up and went over to replenish their glasses. On the face of it, they were glad that Moon had returned, and not solely for the sake of the family treasury. They liked him.

The Professor said, "How was it that Benjamin Franklin put it? Masturbation is its own reward."

Bitter Joe said, "It wasn't Franklin, it was Voltaire and what he said was, 'One push in the bush is worth two in the hand.' "

"What's the slogan of the teenager?" the Doc said, "Ummm. Never put off 'til tomorrow what you can pull on today."

The family was in full swing. Moon was looking from one to the other as though flabbergasted. He had expected a warmer reaction to his traitorous act.

"Beat your meat," the Doc said reminiscently. "That's what we used to call it. Jack it up. But, you know, I think masturbation as an art, or science, or hobby, or whatever you want to call it, has fallen off considerably since I was a boy. It's this new availability of sex from the earliest years."

Moon winced but reapplied himself to his drink. Offhand, he couldn't remember ever having heard such conversation in mixed company, certainly not mixed company that included four-year-old kids.

Rusty said, "The same with sex in general. Christ, in a matter of a couple of decades it went from the Victorian prudery to complete freedom. Wife swapping, group sex, swingers, 51 varieties of Gays. The works. Great. It was surprising how quickly, given complete sexual freedom, people began to yawn at the supposedly far-out. Sex we will undoubtedly always have with us, thank goodness, but doing it whilst swinging from a chandelier probably isn't really enjoyed even by the chimpanzee."

Blackie, who was knitting, said complacently, "I think you're right, dear. Most of the centuries-old sharp desires have had their keen edges worn off. There seem to be few, any longer, who want to have their screwing with sixteen others in the room either participating or watching, or to whip or be whipped, or to bugger or be buggered, for that matter.''

Moon gaped at her. Her appearance, with her knitting and sitting in a rocking chair, was that of a benign, late-middle-aged matron.

''Look,'' he said, largely to change the subject before someone else expanded on the question of the desirability to bugger or be buggered, ''When I first came here we were talking about the current Guaranteed Annual Stipend, and how so many in the country now get it without working, from the day they're eighteen to the grave.''

''Why not?'' Rusty demanded. ''How do the Rockefellers get their stipend, most of them without even making a pretense of working at all, except sometimes figurehead jobs? For at least a century and a half that family has lived in ultimate luxury. Or the DuPonts. Christ, over two centuries of inherited wealth there! Where did it come from? It came from the same place our GAS comes from; the present generation inherited it from past generations. But where's the rest of *our* inheritance? The human race has bequeathed us all its inventions, its developed technology, down through the ages. The wheel, once dreamed up on the steppes of southern Siberia, or wherever, the iron first tempered, cast and worked, from ore by some Hittite, or whoever, was not left to any individual, any family, or even any class or nation. Nor any other invention down through the ages. They're the property of the whole human race. And the race has now gotten to the point where, through the advances made bit by bit, it can produce an abundance for all, with a minimum of labor. But that abundance should belong to the race, not to individuals, not to a few wealthy. As it is, we on GAS get precious little of the human heritage.''

Moon put up a hand to ward off her indignation. "It's not that," he protested. "My gripe against GAS is that we're allowing ourselves to become a race of parasites. We do nothing. It's fine that we've finally solved the production of ample for all, but that doesn't mean we should sit back and retire, except for a handful of useful workers."

Doc looked at him doubtfully, "Ummm. You said you were a biologist. How did it work out for you?"

Moon looked rueful. "I exaggerated that a bit," he admitted, "but I was a victim, I suppose, of the educational half-life."

Ron had returned to his seat from a pilgrimage to the applejack jug. "What's that?" he said.

Moon said, still rueful, "You get out of school, after studying one of the hard sciences and go to work, if the computers select you for a job as a hundred percent expert. In five years, half of everything you learned is antiquated, since knowledge is doubling every eight to ten years. In another five years, half of your remaining knowledge is antiquated. In other words, after 10 years you're only twenty-five per cent expert. It used to be that an M.D. could take his degree in 1925 and remain in practice for the rest of his life, retiring after forty years in 1965, and never having opened a book during that time. No more. A patient these days wouldn't allow you to prescribe aspirin for him, even if you had attempted to keep up and the computers had okayed you. Everybody wants some-body fresh out of the medical schools with all the new techniques."

"Amen," the Doc said, slugging back some of his refined apple juice. "I never did get an appointment."

The Wizard came into the saloon, looking his superiority, and Franny said, "What's new, Richard?"

He said, slumping into a chair with all the grace of a fifteen-year-old, "Not much, Mother. A lot about the Second Constitutional Convention and the Indians. Senator Corksoaker wants to abolish prisons in the new Constitution."

"Senator *who*?"

The youngster shrugged, "Maybe it was Cockstroker," he admitted.

"That can't be his name, dear," Blackie said placidly.

"Why not?" the Professor said. "It's all in the tradition of how last names were originally decided upon. John became John *Smith*, because that was his trade. Henry became Henry Weaver, since that was his trade. Evidently, this senator's ancestors were corksoakers."

"Corksoakers?" JoJo said vaguely. "I suppose I misunderstood what the Wizard called him."

"Of course," the Professor told her. "In early bottling, they used corks. Before they could be inserted in bottles, they had to be properly soaked to a certain degree of softness, but not *too* soft."

"That's right," Bitter Joe nodded. "And a cockstroker was connected with the rooster fights in the old days. His job was to infuriate the fighting rooster immediately before he went into battle, by rubbing his feathers the wrong way or tickling his balls, or whatever."

Bowser said, sotto voce, "How about cokesuckers, for tasters at Cola manufacturers?"

"Shut up," Moon advised him and said to the Wizard, "What was this proposition to abolish prisons?"

The Wizard turned his eyes to the newcomer to the family and said, "The Senator wants to make the prisoners stay at home. He claims that as they are now, the standard of living is slightly higher than that of a single person on the outside on GAS. They've all got spacious cells now, with private bath. Jails are coeducational, or whatever you call it, and you can bunk with whoever you want, or have your boy friend or girl in a couple of times a week. Evidently, the Mexicans pioneered that departure. Kept the prisoners from going stir crazy or homosexual. Oh, the Senator claims there are too many reasons these days for people wanting to be in prison, including getting away from your family and relatives."

The usually quiet Colleen shook her head and said, "I ought to listen to the news more often. What else, Wizard?"

Colleen looked like this: The daughter of the Doc, she had inherited his lardy qualities. Her plain, round face held disillusionment, especially when she eyed the twins, her offspring. She was about twenty-eight, could have passed for five years older. Her legs were too short and her fanny too damned large. The main reason she worked in town at the Ultra-Market was to prove herself, to herself. She got precious little more in pay than if she'd been on GAS. She looked as though at any minute she'd begin mopping the floor, if it needed mopping or not.

The Wizard, pleased at his position as the center of attention, said, "Well, the delegates from the Peace Party want an article in the Revised Constitution abolishing the military. They figure that the original reasons for war are gone. They used to have all sorts of patriotic slogans but the reasons they fought were for land, raw materials, trade outlets and to get slaves. All antiquated. Who wants more territory when population is falling off? And it's cheaper to buy raw materials than to finance a war to rip them off. Manufacture has gotten to the point where practically everybody makes everything himself, so trade has fallen away. And with ninety percent of the population of the world unemployed, who wants slaves?"

"How about fighting to make the world safe for Democracy?" Ron said.

"Been tried already," Zack told him, "but after that war was won there was less democracy than before it started."

Doc said unhappily, "Ummm. But the Second World War was to make the world safe against dictatorship."

"Yeah," Zack said again, "But there were more dictatorships on the side of the Allies than there were on the Axis side."

Bitter Joe said, "We heard stories that young men liked war. They liked to fight."

"Yes, of course we heard such stories," the Professor snorted. "But then why did old men have to draft the young ones?"

"Anything else interesting?" Franny said. "Nobody's come up with a proposal that GAS be abolished and everybody be put back to work on the space program, ecology, in the arts and so forth?"

"Oh, no," the Wizard said with lofty scorn. "You're out of date, Mother. The Reformed Agnostic Church wants to repeal the Ten Commandments. They say it's a set of rules made up for a primitive nomadic people and doesn't apply to our times."

"What in the hell do you mean, dear?" Blackie said placidly.

The Wizard said, "Well, they claim about a third of the Commandments deal with what a great guy God is, and how he's jealous and doesn't want any other gods around, especially graven images, and you've got to keep His sabbath. The Reformed Agnostics say this isn't a very sympathetic picture of a diety, demanding prayer and worship and adulation and all. A pretty vain, primitive figure. Jesus and Mary, toward whom a lot of this prayer has been going more recently, were shy, humble, unassuming types, largely, and would have been embarrassed by all this worship jazz. If it had been up to Jesus, He would have scrapped those parts of the Ten Commandments.''

''Perhaps,'' Colleen said, ''but that doesn't mean you have to throw out all of the rest. How about the other Commandments, such as Honor thy father and thy mother?'' She looked doubtfully at the marauding twins even as she asked.

Bitter Joe took that up, after knocking down another slug of his brandy. ''Why should you?'' he said. ''You didn't ask to be born. You never signed the contract. You're under no obligation. If your father and mother deserve through their actions to be honored and loved, okay. But suppose your father was Hitler and he took on a diseased whore while he was drunk and never even knew you were conceived. When you came along, you were born blind and crippled as a result of the VD and had a hard time, particularly since your mother threw you out on the streets. Now, why in the hell should you honor parents like that?''

The Professor nodded agreement. ''Yes, of course. The Commandment admits to no extenuating circumstances. You honor your father and your mother, period. No matter what they do.''

Ron said, unhappily, ''Well, Thou shalt not kill.''

Bitter Joe snorted. ''Thou shalt not kill what? We're omnivorous animals. If we don't kill other life forms, especially plant life, we starve. Does it mean only humans? But it was God himself who ordered the Hebrews into the

Promised Land with sword and torch to perform such massacres as that at Jericho where they killed not only the male enemy but all the males in town, including donkeys and cattle. The women and children they enslaved.'' He grunted. ''Even in the modern world, sometimes you have to kill. Suppose some crazy sniper is on the top of a roof knocking everybody off in sight? Do you kill him, or not?''

The Doc said, ''Or take 'Neither shalt thou commit adultery.' Well, that's not so easy to follow these days. Nobody bothers to get married anymore, certainly not in the old sense.'' He thought about it. ''Come to think of it, the old Hebrews were not only patriarchal at the time the Commandments were stated, but polygamous as well. In short, they had an extended family—of sorts. But the whole thing was silly, so far as morals were concerned. Remember that Solomon, one example among many, legally, by Jewish religious law, had hundreds of wives. If those wives didn't commit adultery, how did they ever get laid? Or were they all lesbians, or frigid, or what?''

Sweet Alice said wistfully, ''Maybe in those days the men were more . . . well, you know.''

''And they called Solomon a wise man,'' Rusty said sourly. ''Hundreds of wives, yet.''

Zack said, trying to inject a bon mot, ''Well, there's that Commandment where you're not supposed to covet thy neighbor's ass. Certainly took a blow at homosexuality.''

Several of them, including Moon and Franny, bothered to groan.

''As a former women's libber, I object to that Commandment the most,'' Rusty said, mild heat in her voice. ''It's based on private property and lists among other items belonging to your neighbor that you shouldn't covet, his wife and his maidservant. In other words, both were his private property.''

Bowser, who had temporarily been reprieved from the twins, had now clambered upon the Doc's ample lap with malice aforethought. The dog said, "Enough of all this religious crap. Anything else in the news—especially about dogs?''

That got chuckles from most of the family, some of whom looked at Moon, trying to catch his lips moving.

The Professor looked over at the Wizard and said, "What about the Indians?''

The Wizard was happily in the limelight again. He pushed his horn-rims back on the bridge of his nose. "It's all a confused mess," he said. "For one thing, they've all seemed to disappear except for Buffalo Dong and his braves. They materialize from time to time and pull off something, and then fade back into the woodwork.''

"Such as what, dear?'' Blackie said.

"Such as pour a couple of barrels of conductive salts solution into the Guaranteed Annual Stipend computers just south of Denver. The government handled the whole southwest from there. But some say it wasn't them at all. Some say it was a gang of malcontents who weren't eligible to get on GAS and some say it was members of the Posterity Party.''

Moon looked up sharply. "The what?''

The Wizard was lofty. "You've probably never heard of them. They're the only party not at the Second Constitutional Convention. They don't like GAS.''

"What else about the Apaches?'' the Doc asked, around the harassment of the twins.

"The Swiss have offered to mediate.''

Everyone looked at him.

"What in the world are they going to mediate?" Franny said.

"The war. It's traditional with Switzerland. They offer to preside at a peace conference between the Marijuaneros and the United States of the Americas. Our government is pissed off at them. Says it's an internal affair and none of their business."

"What else have the Apaches done?" Sweet Alice said, wide-eyed.

"Nothing much, really," the Wizard told her with his hair-tearing, irksome tone of superiority. "The rumors about where they are are endless. The Air Force bombed another bridge they thought they were crossing, but it was only a troop of Boy Scouts and they all dived into the water just in time but the bridge is a washout and they have to re-route traffic and . . ."

"What'd ya mean, another bridge?" Zack said.

"Oh, they've bombed various things. And what they don't bomb the National Guard is shelling, or trampling down with their tanks."

"Good grief. Well, where *are* the Apaches?" the Professor said.

"Nobody knows. They've disappeared into the hills, the deserts, maybe the small towns, for all General Peterflogger seems to know."

Bitter Joe said, "I get the picture. Every Indian in the southwest is for them. And a helluva lot of whites, probably. Do-gooders, bleeding hearts, and people who're down on the government for whatever reason. That sort of thing. It's the old story. Robin Hood, Pretty Boy Floyd, Jesse and Frank James. Or, on a larger scale, the guerrillas in Yugoslavia, Mao's communists, or the Viet Cong in the Asian War for that matter."

"What in the dickens are you talking about?" Ron said, making a new onslaught on the applejack jug as if it contained glue for this fragmented conversation.

Bitter Joe said, "They had their work cut out catching Robin Hood, Pretty Boy or Jesse James because the locals knew what side of their bread the butter was on. Those guys split their loot with the poor. The same with Tito and his guerrillas and the others. They had the people on their side and could go to ground whenever they had to. You can't keep up a guerrilla operation without the support of the people."

It went on into the night, the advent of a stranger such as Moon always being a family treat. From time to time, the spirit would move someone to go off and attend to a farm chore, such as milking the goats, ushering the rest of the livestock back into The Barn, or getting the twins to bed. Doc and Franny disappeared for awhile into the kitchen to prepare the evening meal. Franny had picked up a couple of dishes in the East which she wanted to demonstrate to the family chef and gourmet.

Nobody was feeling any pain, nor was there a dearth of subjects to be debated. Moon's mind reeled from more than the apple brandy.

At last, long after the last morsel of Franny's supper was a pungent memory, and the dishes done up by whomever the spirit moved (to everyone's surprise, this included Ruthie), they began to melt away to bed, one by one, or two by two—as the spirit moved.

Sweet Alice, her eyes wide with characteristic innocence, said to Moon, "Where are you going to sleep?"

"With me," Franny told her flatly.

And shortly after that, Moon and Franny said their goodnights to those remaining and went on out to her hover-car, which she had parked in the garage of the underground dwelling, to get their luggage. Bowser brought up the rear.

As they pulled things from the vehicle, Moon said to her, "I'll take in my voco-typer. I want to take some notes down before I forget them."

She looked at him. "Working already?"

He shook his head in wonderment and told her, "This bunch is further around the bend than any I've ever come up against. But some of them have some fascinating opinions. And this is America at the working level. In fact, to my surprise, after your description, I find their average intelligence and grasp damned high. Always excluding that dizzy blonde."

"Sweet Alice," Franny supplied. "In the old days she would have made a perfect call girl. She would have loved the work."

". . . and Zack, even Zack isn't stupid. Just young—or something."

They started back for the patio, Bowser leading the way now.

Franny said, "Did you check the house for bugging? You never know."

"Yes. At least the saloon and Ron's room, where I'm sleeping. Nothing." He added with a plaintive note: "What's all this about you calling the Wizard 'Richard', and his calling you mother?"

"Nothing simpler: That's his name, and I'm his mother."

"You are?" He was mildly surprised. "Any idea who his father is?"

"I haven't the vaguest. I was going with several men at the time. He was born shortly after I joined the family. I was in bad shape at that time. I stayed here for a couple of years in a row.''

Moon shook his head as they entered the room he'd been in the night before. He said, ''Then you really are a member of this off-beat group?''

''Uh-huh. At least, I identify with them more than anyone else. Whenever I get tired of helling around, or getting involved in crackpot socioeconomic movements, I come to recuperate here.''

He put down his oversized suitcase and the portable voco-typer he was carrying and looked over at her. ''Why don't you donate to them a sizable chunk of pseudo-dollar credits?''

''Because they don't need it,'' she said reasonably. ''They're leading a good life. If they had a lot of money laid on them out of a clear sky, they'd probably just blow it on something they don't really want—such as a talking dog.'' She put down her own luggage and said, ''Which reminds me. That was a silly little trick to pull.''

He shrugged and grinned. ''No, it wasn't. It was protective coloring and I knew you'd catch up with me. Now they've got me typed: an amateur con artist. They couldn't dream of my being anything else. And you were right. This is an ideal place for me to go to ground.''

She was exasperated. ''You damn fool. Don't you see that switching the family's total account to your phony one in the National Data Bank's Banking Section will appear on the records and some very rough types will know what vicinity you're in? I don't think you realize how vicious the Bureau of Investigation can be. Haven't you ever read of the CIA and FBI in the old days? They'd pull anything —up to and including the overthrow of governments or the assassination of foreign leaders, not to speak of dumping three-ton bilivits on American citizens that the powers in control didn't like.''

"Fine, fine," Moon said, flinging his bag to one of the two beds and opening it so that he could get his night things. "But I didn't spend anything, and I doubt if they'll check out the transaction between Zack and me and back again, within days. Besides, there's no particular reason to believe they've cracked this new identity that Dick Jennings came up with.''

"If they haven't, they will," Franny said darkly.

Moon began unbuttoning his shirt and changed the subject. "Did you check out the neighborhood?''

"Thoroughly. There's precious little to check, save for Coronado. This is really the American boondocks.''

"What if something happens to you, heaven forbid, or we become separated, or whatever?''

"Our sole contact in the immediate area is a Party member in Coronado. He was once a registered Democratic-Republican and it's unlikely that anyone knows he's changed parties. His name is Max Cohn. He's a young fellow who is in government employ, locally in charge of the administration of Guaranteed Annual Stipend. If anything happens to me, go and reveal yourself to him.''

"He knows who I am?''

"Of course, if he's a Party member. But I didn't mention you to him. He doesn't know that you're in these parts. Even in Party ranks, the fewer who know about your location, the better. But so far as we know, nothing will happen to me—for the present. Not even old Roy Thomas would suspect a member of the rocket-set to be fronting for you.''

"We hope," he said, crawling into bed. He sighed as

his head hit the pillow. "What does that old dipsomaniac, Doc, make his applejack out of; liquid plutonium?"

"Apples," she said, crawling in beside him. "I should have checked your intake. When you're drunk, you snore."

"Drunk!" he said indignantly. "I never get so drunk that I can't hang onto the floor."

Chapter Eleven

The town of Coronado, New Mexico, was an anachronism.

It was discovered by Pedro de Tovar, one of Coronado's lieutenants, in 1541, twenty years after Cortes had taken Montezuma's Tenochtitlan and liquidated the Aztec power. De Tovar reported to Coronado that the pueblo had a population of over ten thousand and that he had captured it in a desperate fray. But his chief, in reporting back to Mexico City, proved that he was cut from the same cloth as Hernan Cortes himself, who had, let us say, rendered a somewhat erroneous report on the size and magnificence of Montezuma's capital in his dispatches to Spain. Coronado fudged the population figure up to 20,000, though he hadn't seen the pueblo that was eventually to bear his name.

In actuality, the settlement of pueblo Indians had never numbered more than two thousand peaceable folk who had fled the prairies for this mountain region to escape the attacks of the more warlike Comanches. It hadn't grown much by the turn of the 21st Century.

Throughout its history, following the coming of the Spanish, Coronado had always been less than an affluent metropolis. Its single claim to a period of prosperity had come when the Mountain Men, fur traders, had for six years made it their annual rendezvous with their year's catch of furs to sell and to get smashed in celebration, to get laid and to purchase their supplies for the coming year.

By the time the United States, undoubtedly motivated by altruistic reasons, had liberated Texas, New Mexico, Arizona and California, in the mid-19th Century, Coronado had largely become the town it was ever to be.

The coming of the Ultra-Welfare State, People's Capitalism, or what you will, had been a disaster to local enterprise—if there had ever been any. With the exception of a few small sheltered valleys, a few acres here and there with sources of water, agriculture had always been a fruitless thing in the vicinity. With the advent of Guaranteed Annual Stipend, it became a farce. A margin farmer does not even attempt to work his twenty or thirty acres when the best he can expect for the fruit of his toil is less than a third what the government will give him free, without backbreaking labor. The very thought of modern agricultural methods, utilizing automated farm equipment, was a cynic's laugh. There was no land suitable for megacredit farming within a hundred miles of Coronado.

Such farming as there had been was the only source of income to the backwash town. With the coming of automation, such subsidiary jobs that once existed fell off to the point where the total work force numbered no more than a double score, most of them government employees. No longer were there even jobs putting cans on supermarket shelves; the Ultra-Market was automated and serviced from Sante Fe to the south. The sole restaurant was an Auto-Cafeteria, requiring neither chef, kitchen help nor waitresses. The sole service station was also automated. Such mechanical work as was required at the government-operated Auto-Pool, where vehicles could be rented, also came up from Sante Fe. There were no local garages otherwise. The one hotel, and the one motel, on the outskirts, needed neither maids nor reception clerks any more than the one local theater required ticket sellers, takers or ushers. Not in these days of automation.

In short, for all practical purposes there were no jobs through which the ambitious could provide themselves with income beyond the government dole. A few office workers, administrators in the various distribution projects, were all that were required. Even two of the local bars were automated; only the third, locally owned, boasted a live bartender.

Those with ambition, born in Coronado, left; many of them to return when they found that the balance of the United States of the Americas didn't offer much more in the way of opportunity.

Upshot: It was one drab, godawfully meaningless town.

Which didn't detract from bitterness in the hearts of the locals. And since they had little else toward which to direct their enmity, they took it out on the handful of soul-farms which had sprung up in the outlying areas, such as that of the Chutzpa family.

For GAS wasn't enough for the dreams of the average resident of Coronado. The Tri-Di shows which occupied a sizable portion of their time provided them with examples aplenty of how life could be and should be. They were well aware how the rocket-set lived. They knew all

too well—through the media—how the stars of New Hollywood and the Tri-Di world pleasured themselves. They
saw the commercials for the swank, speedy, privately
owned hover-cars, the yachts, the deluxe hotels and
restaurants, the gadgets, the fabulous clothes, jewelries,
perfumes and all the rest of the latest fashions. They knew
all about travel to exotic lands—but only via the media.
They even knew about travel-now-pay-later, not that there
was going to be a later in which they were more finan-
cially solvent, and credit organizations eyed them dimly if
they bothered to apply. Theirs was a hand-me-down
existence.

What teed them off so far as such groups as the Chutzpas were concerned was that the family, on the face of it,
didn't give a damn for the goodies of the rocket-set. They
clearly didn't mind dressing in denims and homemade
sandals, when they wore footwear at all. (In season, a
New Mexico 'goathead' thorn could penetrate heavy armor.)
They didn't mind eating their own produce, rather than the
latest in frozen or canned delectable foods, as advertised
on Tri-Di. They obviously didn't yearn for speedy privately owned hover-cars, but were satisfied to rent from the
Auto-Pool whenever they required a vehicle. They didn't
even mind bootlegging and drinking their own guzzle,
rather than the internationally advertised brands of superior
booze up to and including champagne, not that anyone in
Coronado had ever sampled champagne.

On top of it all, unbelievably, those Chutzpa bastards
seemed to be happy in their deprived lives. Happy, mind
you!

It was a supposedly well-known fact that some of these
members of extended families were rich and that they
could, if they chose, buy the luxuries desired by all but

idiots, but had no desire to. This was what was so infuriating. The citizens of Coronado didn't particularly resent the rich (as depicted on the Tri-Di shows) having things they did not, but they *loathed* the idea of somebody being able to have such things and scorning them. How could these mad folk put up with going barefoot during the early summer, when available to them were the latest swank shoes from Italy? It was quite unbearable.

Thus it was that members of the Chutzpa family avoided going into Coronado except when necessary. The town offered nothing that might have otherwise attracted them, but putting up with snide remarks, catcalls, sneers from the unemployed young bums who hung out on the corners of the Coronado plaza, was too much to bother with. There was no point in adding to the surly atmosphere. Who could tell? It wasn't out of the realm of possibility that one of the malcontents might post himself on a nearby hill with a twenty-two rifle and a hun's mentality, and plink at the glass of the solar collectors in Sun Valley. Twenty rounds of ammunition could have wreaked havoc.

So it was that when JoJo entered town to see about getting on the Guaranteed Annual Stipend rolls, she was dressed demurely by family standards and made her way directly to the city hall, which faced the plaza. The city hall was one of the few two-story buildings in town and one of the few not constructed of adobe brick. This left-over from New Deal days had been built with WPA funds, back when the government was desperately seeking ways in which to reduce unemployment, and hadn't come up as yet with Negative Income Tax, not to speak of GAS. It was in pseudo-Spanish Colonial style, and, on the face of it, the government's architect had never seen so much as a map of Spain. His ideas on Spanish Colonial had been drawn from movie sets, the designers of which had also never gotten around to seeing the land from which the Conquistadores hailed.

Running only a comparatively mild gauntlet of wolf whistles and murmured invitations to bed from the plaza palookas, JoJo entered the building and without undue difficulty located the offices of the Guaranteed Annual Stipend Administration. Offices, because there were two of them, an outer reception room, bare and drab in the tradition of government reception rooms in minor towns, and an inner office presided over by Max Cohn, sole representative of the administration for a considerable distance, his regional office being in Albuquerque, over a hundred miles to the southeast.

JoJo approached the auto-receptionist sitting on the room's lone desk and asked the screen for an appointment. There wasn't anyone else present, but she was told to be seated. She obeyed orders, found a straight chair and sat demurely, hands in her lap. It was her first confrontation with bureaucracy but JoJo had poise in her chromosomes.

At least fifteen minutes passed before the autoreceptionist said, "Ms. JoJo Chutzpa," and the door behind and to one side of the reception desk opened.

JoJo stood, said meaninglessly to the auto-receptionist, "Thank you," and marched in.

The office beyond was larger than that which she had first entered and not quite so drab. Not quite.

At the desk a young man sat, seemingly absorbed in the papers before him. For the moment, he didn't deign to look up. He cleared his throat, striving for importance, and said in a voice meant to hold a trace of the brusque, "Sit down, I'll be with you in a moment."

JoJo seated herself again and folded her hands in her lap.

Max Cohn looked up at long last and stared; his prominent Adam's apple bobbed.

For she was a dove with dove's eyes. And she was the Rose of Sharon and the lily of the valley. And the voice of the turtle was heard in the land.

Max Cohn looked like this: He was about twenty-five and his doting family had raised him to be a scholar-intellectual. Although in appearance he didn't quite come up to the ideal, still he bore a trace of it. He was too thin and his eyes were sad and his nose was of the shape that once inspired Nazi cartoonists. He was only an inch or two taller than JoJo and beyond that there could be no outward similarity whatsoever save that they were both members of the human race. He looked like Anthony Perkins playing the part of a confused inmate of Dachau.

He looked as though he needed encouragement, so JoJo smiled at him encouragingly.

Max Cohn gulped and got out, "Uh . . . uh, what? That is, what can I, uh, do for you?"

And the vision said, "I came to apply for GAS."

Max Cohn was new to the job, which was a reason for his ineptness, one of the reasons he had tried to establish his authority by having her wait in the outer office. One of the reasons he had pretended business when she had first entered. To be frank, he knew precious little about just what he was doing here. It had come as a shock when, upon his graduation from the University City of Albuquerque, the computers had chosen him for a position with the Guaranteed Annual Stipend Administration. It had also come as a mild surprise to his superiors at regional headquarters. They had already put through a recommendation that the Coronado office be discontinued and that the area it served be turned over to Sante Fe, or Taos.

But, unknown to Max Cohn, his dossier in the National Data Banks indicated that he was registered as a Democratic-Republican, as had been his parents, and his grandparents. His great-grandparents had all been Republicans, before the merging of the two parties, when at long last it had become obvious to everyone that there was no basic difference between them. On top of his political affiliations, the computers found that young Cohn belonged to one of the oldest families in New Mexico. His ancestor, indeed, had first arrived with the expedition from Mexico City which had given Coronado its name. And providentially, at that. When the physician Pedro Cohn, once of Málaga, Spain, had joined in the search for the golden cities of Cibola, his timing was such that he barely anticipated the arrival of the Spanish Inquisition in New Spain. He was sensible enough not to return south toward the tender loving care of the torturers.

But although this information was in the data banks, it was not in the knowledge of Max Cohn, nor had it been in that of his late parents. Nor was it in the knowledge of his contemporaries in Coronado. In short, he might belong to the oldest family in town, and be of impeccable political background, but nobody knew it and certainly his family name carried no prestige. To his fellow townsmen he was, as had been his father before him, that Jew bastard. Time offers no escape. Nor does interbreeding, over the centuries, with Indians, Mexicans, and Americans of British, French and German descent. One of Max's paternal ancestors should have changed his name from Cohn to Smith. Every last one of those ancestors could have answered Shakespeare's question. What's in a name? Bigotry.

Max did his best to rally, considering the emotional pressures he was under. "Gas?" he said.

JoJo smiled. "Bitter Joe says that in the old days, it was a slang term. They'd say, 'It's a gas.' You know, Guaranteed Annual Stipend. Isn't this the office?"

"Oh. Oh, yes, of course. Absolutely." He fumbled in a drawer of his desk. This was his first new application since taking over the job. He rose to the occasion. "Now then Ms., ah, Chutzpa . . ." He came to a halt and stared down reproachfully at the paper upon which he had noted her name. "Chutzpa?" he said again. "That can't be right. That's a Yiddish term meaning . . ."

She smiled again, all but flooring him, and said, "No. That's right. When the family amalgamated, for the sake of efficiency, everybody changed their name to Chutzpa. I think that it was Bitter Joe who thought of it."

Max shook his head infinitesimally to clear it and took up a stylo.

"Uh, very well, Ms., uh, Chutzpa. As an American citizen you are eligible to apply for Guaranteed Annual Stipend upon reaching the age of eighteen, if you are without employment. Now, then, just how old are you?"

JoJo said, "I think I'll be about nineteen, come next corn festival."

"Next corn festival?"

Her laugh actually tinkled. He had read the term as applied to laughter but had never heard it before. Now he heard it.

She said, "We grow sweet corn as well as some field corn and when the sweet corn becomes ripe we have a festival, like the Iroquois up in New York used to have before the white men came. And we simply gorge ourselves on sweet corn. Bet you didn't know it's delicious even without cooking. Did you know that you shouldn't boil fresh corn more than three minutes?''

"No," he said weakly. Max Cohn had never been smitten before. Desperately he wanted for her to continue talking. She could have recited from a telephone directory without losing his attention.

"Well, for three days we eat sweet corn and what we can't eat we can." She made a cute moue in apology for the humor attempt . . . which had passed him by, at any rate. "And, about the same time, string beans and lima beans. And we combine them sometimes and make succotash."

Max cleared his throat. He had nearly fainted, watching her mouth say 'succotash.' "It must be wonderful. I'd like to come."

"Oh, why don't you? We just love visitors at corn festival time. Usually friends from some of the other soul-farms."

He looked at her, trying not to do it hungrily. Max Cohn had heard about the loose ways of the extended families on the soul-farms. He wasn't sure what she meant by loving visitors, but he wrenched his thoughts away from what he hoped she meant. Max Cohn was a virgin—but he dreamt.

He brought himself back to the present. "Yes, yes, of course." He cleared his throat, still once again, the adam's apple bobbing desperately. "Now, how do you mean you think you'll be about nineteen? What was your birthdate?"

Her smile was dazzling. "I'm not sure. I was awfully young at the time."

"But . . . but . . . well, everybody knows their birthday. Didn't your parents tell you?"

"I don't have any parents."

He looked at her with compassion. "You mean they're both dead?"

"I don't know," she explained, winningly. "You see, I was born just a few months before my mother—my mother's name was Nora . . . I think—joined the family. And after we became Chutzpas she decided she didn't like it very much, the farm and all, and she kind of wandered off and nobody knows where she went. At least, I don't think anybody does. Maybe Blackie does. She kind of keeps up on that sort of thing."

"But, you mean she just abandoned you?" Max Cohn, who had been raised in a much more orthodox surrounding, was appalled.

"Oh, no." JoJo was contrite over giving the wrong impression. "I was with the family. They raised me. With Sweet Alice and Zack and Ron, but the boys are kind of older."

"Now, just a moment, please. Uh, what was your mother's original name?"

It was her turn to look blank.

He said, an element of desperation there, "Well, what was your father's name?"

"Oh, mother probably didn't know who he was."

He stared down at the application blank in dismay. "You mean, you don't know either your true father's or your true mother's last name?"

She smiled charmingly at his perception. "That's right," she said with a brightness that would have done credit to Sweet Alice.

"Well, were they American citizens?"

"How would I know?"

"But—where were you born, ah, where was your birth certificate registered?"

She looked at him emptily. "Does that matter?"

"Matter? Ms. Chutzpa, if your parents weren't Americans, or if you weren't born in the United States of the Americas, then you're not eligible for Guaranteed Annual Stipend."

"Oh, dear," she sighed. "I was afraid that something might go wrong." She came to her feet, graceful as the fawn she was. "The family will be disappointed. We were all waiting for me to be eighteen, so I could contribute my share of GAS to the family account. Well, anyway, thank you Mr. . . ."

He was aghast. "You mean, now they'll throw you out?"

She blinked at him. "Why would they do that? I'm a member of the family."

He stumbled to his feet, nearly knocking his chair over backward. He held out a hand in her direction. "Oh, now, wait!"

She paused and looked at him, still obviously puzzled at his last words.

Something entirely beside the point occurred to him, inanely. "Uh," he said. "You wouldn't know your, uh, religious, or, uh, that is, *racial* background. . . ?"

She looked at him blankly. "I don't believe I have any."

"No, no, of course not," he said miserably. Deep within him, he knew very well that she couldn't be a Jewish girl, good or otherwise.

She turned to go again but he said hurriedly, "Now, wait. Possibly there's something we can do."

"What?"

"Well, surely there's someone out at your, uh, family. Someone who knew your mother. Would know her origi- nal last name. Then we could check her back through the data banks. Find out where you were born. Then everything would be . . . clear.''

She thought about that and he loved the tiny wrinkle that thinking developed in her forehead. Such a forehead. A marble sculpture; a Grecian goddess!

Then the warmth of that devastating smile was boiling his brain again. ''Would it be possible for you to come out? Any time would do. Perhaps Blackie, or Rusty, or the Doc or Professor might remember something. But it seems so much trouble for you.''

He resisted swooning at this opportunity to see more of the woman he loved.

Chapter Twelve

Buffalo Dong and Marcy stood back aways in the trees from the clearing in the wood which led up to the mountain lodge. They surveyed it thoughtfully.

Marcy said, "From what we could see from the heliohopper we ripped off, it's the only house within ten miles in any direction."

"Yeah," he said. "Everybody's pulling out. Hysterical. I'm surprised these stayed. I can't make out any wires. Probably there aren't any. Too far to the nearest power source. They'd use power packs for lights, refrigeration and all."

Marcy said, "Hank'll give us the word on that. He's the electrical engineer. I wonder where the boys are. They're taking an awful long time."

But with that Jim Aravaipa slithered around a tree and was next to them.

"God damn it all," Buffalo Dong blurted. "Don't

do that. You'll scare me out of my current bout of diarrhea.''

Jim grinned at him and said, ''I thought you were the big Green Beret back in the Asian War.''

''Yeah, well that was over thirty years ago,'' the older man snarled. ''I haven't even been squirrel hunting since then. What's up there?''

''Hank's around at the rear, guarding the back door. He can also see the garage, so they couldn't get out that way. They've got a late model hover-limo. By the looks of the garden and so forth there aren't any kids, and by the size of the house there's probably not more than two or three adults. There's French windows going into the side from the garden. I can enter that way.''

''All right,'' Buffalo Dong said. ''Let's get into our costumes.'' He looked accusingly at Marcy. ''I still think you should put on war paint.''

''Screw you, Jack,'' she said.

The two men fished into their large leather pouches and came up with black wigs which hung down to their shoulders, in somewhat grimy disarray. They put these on and then tied leather thongs around their foreheads. Marcia Kintpuash put a suede band, decorated with turquoise, around her own brows, making her look somewhat reminiscent of Minne-Ha-Ha.

''How about the war paint?'' Jim said unhappily.

''Sure, war paint,'' the chief growled, bringing forth a jar of grease paint from his possibles sack.

''The damn stuff takes a month of Tuesdays to get off.''

''It's part of the image. You want to look like a blood-thirsty Apache, don't you?''

''My mother wanted me to be a violinist,'' Jim muttered, bringing forth his own grease paint.

"We'll move in fast," the chief instructed Jim Aravaipa. "We don't want them to be able to get to a TV phone."

"Right." Jim moved off, letting his laser rifle slip from his shoulder into his hands.

Buffalo Dong and the girl moved to the point where the trees came nearest to the front door, then quickly broke cover and hurried for the log-constructed vacation lodge.

The door wasn't locked. They burst through and into a long, comfortable living room. It was in the epitome of style according to publications devoted to holiday and weekend houses. In short, it was done in Effete Rustic.

At their moment of entrance, Hank burst in from the rear, and Jim through the French windows from the garden. Both of the younger men had their weapons at the ready, and their eyes darted around as though looking for targets.

"Ugh," Buffalo Dong said. "White man and squaw our prisoners."

The white man and squaw were sitting comfortably before the enormous fireplace. There was no fire at this time of the year but the room's furniture was organized as if a fire were blazing. He was on a couch, she in a large comfort chair. Drinks were at hand.

Their eyes grew saucer-round.

They looked like this: They were prosperous senior citizens of the not-quite-at-the-top-of-the-heap level. She was short, plumpish, gray of hair and false of teeth, and she wore too much make-up. He was tall and not at all bald, in this day of hair restoration, and looked as though in his time he had gotten used to having his orders obeyed—no matter how stupid. They were dressed in what they probably considered their comfortable, getting-away-from-it-all-in-Injun-country garb.

And neither had ever seen an Indian in their lives,

outside of Tri-Di historical shows, or perhaps at a souvenir stand on the edge of the Grand Canyon. But they knew an Indian when they saw one. You could see that. They knew what Indians looked like. Especially bloodthirsty ones wearing war paint.

"Oh, dear," the white squaw said, and pretended to faint, unable to think of anything else to do.

The man came to his feet, abruptly, albeit clumsily. "You can't do this!" he said in indignation.

"Ugh. What?" Buffalo Dong said stoically. Oh, you could see he was an Apache, all right, all right.

That stopped the white man momentarily. "Well," he said, maintaining the indignation. "Break into my house. Threaten my wife and myself."

"Ugh," Jim said. "No threaten, so far."

Marcy said, "Ugh. Are you two the only ones here?"

"Why . . . why, yes. What is the meaning of this . . . ?"

"Shut um up," Buffalo Dong ordered. He turned to Jim and Hank. "Ugh. Case um house."

The two younger warriors left, Hank trying to suppress a snort. "Case um house," he repeated under his breath. "Jesus! I wish Humphrey Bogart could hear that."

Marcy went over to the window overlooking the road that wound down the mountainside. There was nothing in sight that moved. She hadn't expected there to be; the location was really quite remote.

Buffalo Dong looked at his male captive thoughtfully. "Ugh," he said. "How old are you?"

"Why . . . why, I'm sixty-three. Now, see here, you can't get away with this."

"Shut um up," the Indian commanded.

The elderly white man shut um up.

Jim and Hank returned from their inspection of the rest of the house. Jim said, "Ugh. All clear."

Buffalo Dong looked at the white woman, who had recovered from her supposed faint and was now eyeing them fearfully, though not nearly so much as before. He decided that he'd better throw a scare into her before she began to get ideas.

He said, "How old squaw?"

It was beyond her years of duplicity to refrain from a smirk. "I'm fifty-five."

"Ugh. Too bad."

"What do you mean?" the man demanded. He had sunk back into the seat he had evacuated when the intruders first burst in. He also was beginning to show more signs of truculence.

Buffalo Dong turned eyes to him. "War Council of Marijuanero Apaches has ruled braves not kill unarmed civilians over age of sixty. You go free. Not squaw."

The woman's eyes were popping anew. "You . . . you mean. . . ?"

"Ugh-huh."

She was on her feet, squealing. "But . . . but . . ." She shrilled, "I'm really sixty-four. I was just . . . just fooling." Her eyes darted to the expressionless Marcy. "You . . . you . . . know what I mean."

Marcy looked at her without compassion. "Ugh, no." she said. "My heart is pumping piss for you."

The woman darted back to the older Indian, the obvious leader, and hung onto his arm, desperately. "I can prove it! I can prove it! On my Universal Credit Card and identification. It's all there. Everything. It tells everything."

Buffalo Dong stared at her, disbelief on his usually stoic Indian face. "Get um," he said.

She started for a rear room.

"Don't try gettum away," Buffalo Dong said. "Apache braves all around house. They treat um squaw real rough."

She gasped and darted into a rear bedroom to emerge almost immediately with her papers.

"See . . . see," she said, hysterical triumph in her voice. "I'm really sixty-four. I'm too old to shoot."

"Ugh." Jim said. "White squaw talk with three-forked tongue. Shoot-um anyway."

Buffalo Dong looked at the two prisoners. "We'll see-um," he said. "You two go back in kitchen; cook lots of chuck for Apache braves. We stay in here. You knock plenty loud before you come in. Later, maybe we let you go. Ugh. You never know, with Injun."

The two, supporting each other, headed for the kitchen, which was connected to the far end of the room.

When they were gone, Hank headed over for a cabinet against the wall and opened it up. He had guessed right. "Hey," he said to the others. "Booze! What'd'ya know?"

"You mean 'firewater,' fool," said Jim. "Hell of an Indian you are."

Marcy was looking at Jim. "What in the devil's a three-forked tongue?"

The boy grinned at her. "I'll tell you that right after *you* tell *me*, what does ugh mean?"

"Ugh," she said. "I can see you flunked your Indian philology."

"They got any Scotch?" Buffalo Dong called over to Hank.

"They got everything."

"Let's all have a drink," the leader said. "Now, where in the hell's their National Data Bank Library Booster screen?"

"It's over here," Marcy said. "If they've got ice, make mine rum and coke. Holy mackerel, could I use a drink."

"Get the last few days of news broadcasts," Buffalo Dong said. "Just a summary. The hell with the details."

The four pulled up chairs and faced the Library Booster screen. Marcy fiddled with the dials.

"I hope they've got some good shots of me, from my graduation or someplace," Jim said, taking a good gulp of his beer. "My sainted old mother up in Chicago would like it."

"Shut up," Marcy said testily. "I hope they haven't got good shots of any of us. How long can this go on? We're going to have to ditch that helio-hopper we ripped off. They'll be onto it." She fiddled some more. "Here we are."

The headline went: *Armed Squaws Join Apache Braves In Combat.*

"Armed squaws?" Marcy said, staring at the screen.

"That's you," Buffalo Dong said complacently, taking a slug of the Scotch Hank had brought him. "Hot damn, this is the real thing. I haven't had guzzle like this for . . ."

March said, "What'd'ya mean, that's me?"

"You're the armed squaws. When we captured those two State Troopers, you were toting a holstered pistol."

"Why, those bastards! I'm the Medical Corps."

"Okay, okay," Hank said. "Let's see the news summary."

The headline went: *Refugees Fleeing Arizona and New Mexico. Roads Clogged. Apache Bands Everywhere. San Whiskey, Dorango and New Gomorrah in Flames.*

Jim rubbed the bottom of his face in total disbelief. "In flames?" he said. "How? What the hell are they talking about?"

Buffalo Dong said patiently, "It's the old wartime story. The cops and firemen clear out of town along with everybody else. Then the looters start zeroing in. Not just kids, but adults too. They can do it better, particularly ex-firemen and ex-cops. Then some fire starts, probably by some crackpot vandal on purpose or by a looter by mistake, and it spreads. And you can always blame it on the enemy—us, in this case."

"Gee. I hope nobody gets hurt," Hank said. "Anybody want a repeat on his drink?"

They gave up the hope of a bloodless coup after the next news release.

The National Guard, the vigilantes, the State Police and the Air Force, under command of General Peterflogger, utilizing brilliant strategy and tactics going back to Civil War days, had completely surrounded the largest body of Apache tribesmen. Going in for the kill, they opened fire—in all directions. There had been, at latest count, twenty-six casualties, including five Tri-Di newscameramen. Happily, there had been no fatalities and most of the wounds were minor. The President of the United States of the Americas had awarded each casualty a Purple Heart and a War Cross. All participants in the combat were issued an Indian War Campaign Ribbon, a decoration which hadn't been awarded in well over a century. General "Mad Dog" Peterflogger was granted the Distinguished Service Cross for gallantry beyond the call of duty. The Apaches had escaped the trap without suffering any casualties whatsoever, though the general hinted darkly that they had most likely carried off their dead and wounded to be buried secretly, in the age-old custom of Indian warriors. One of the news commentators unkindly suggested that there hadn't been any Apaches within a hundred miles, and was immediately fired by the National Tri-Di Broadcasting Company.

"Cripes," Jim said. "Twenty-six casualties. They must've shot the hell out of each other."

Hank said, his voice worried, "Listen. You know, this is getting dangerous. There's about fifty thousand trigger-happy jerks running around this part of the country trying to find an Indian to shoot. It's worse than deer season."

"Fifty thousand, my ass," Buffalo Dong said. "There must be at least twice that, and more pouring in every day. But that's what we wanted, wasn't it?"

"Yeah, but how about the poor slobs on the other reservations? The other Apache tribes and the Navahos and Zunis."

"They won't have to worry," the chief said. "Each one of them'll have two or three soldiers guarding him. They couldn't be safer in their mothers' arms. I'll bet every sob-sister reporter, every do-gooder, every bleeding-heart, every Civil Liberties devotee, is already in the southwest protecting the innocent."

There was a loud knock at the kitchen door and Jim went back to it. He ushered in their cowering host and hostess, both of whom bore trays.

"Ugh," Buffalo Dong complained. "Sandwiches. Apache chief and braves getting heap tired of damned sandwiches."

"Apache squaw, too," Marcy muttered. "We haven't had anything but sandwiches for a week."

The white woman said fearfully, "I'm cooking steaks, but they'll take a few minutes. If you'll just wait. I thought this would tide you over. Paté, caviar and smoked salmon."

Hank tightened his mouth to hold back the drooling and grabbed for the nearest sandwich.

Their host was staring at the black-labeled bottle of

Scotch which now sat on a cocktail table, near the library screen. "Hey," he said, in protest. "That's my last bottle of Glengrant. It's worth its weight in diamonds."

Jim intoned, "Ugh. The Great Spirit giveth and the Great Spirit taketh away." As an afterthought, he added, "The Great Spirit is an Indian giver." He reached out for the bottle and poured himself another slug.

Buffalo Dong said to the two terrified whites, "Ugh. You go back into kitchen. Cookum steaks."

The two scurried.

Marcy looked at the chief. "Cookum, yet," she said in disgust, and turned back to the screen for more news from the past few days.

A lieutenant colonel of Intelligence was being interviewed. His face was on the wan side. It turned out that the two State troopers to whom Buffalo Dong had issued the declaration of war, and who had then been scalped with the electric razors, had been able to give enough information on the armament of the three Apaches who had ambushed them to indicate that the guns they carried were the latest Russian laser assault rifles. The lieutenant colonel, looking very unhappy, revealed that this model laser rifle was capable of slicing through a locomotive, or a heavy tank, at almost any distance. It could, he revealed, also slice through a bridge, steel or otherwise, or a small skyscraper.

Buffalo Dong snorted. "That'll give them something to worry about," he said. "Supposedly, the Soviets aren't selling any of these even to their satellites. See what you can get, Marcy, on foreign reaction to our position."

Marcy fiddled with the dials and went back several days.

"Student demonstrations," she said. "Just about everywhere. The students haven't had it so good since Vietnam.

They're all pro-Apache, except Saudi Arabia, South Africa, Morocco and Greece. Oh, and Chile. Don't they have any Indians in Chile?''

"No," Hank said. "The Spanish, uh, *liberated* them all back when they first took over. Fatally."

Marcy said, "Here's something. Frank and his group, over in France."

Frank Barboncito and three other Marijuaneros, including two young women, had applied for political asylum among the French. They were all students at the Sorbonne, studying for their doctorates in political science. They contended that their lives would be in danger if they were returned to the United States of the Americas. They cited statistics proving that the Apaches in America had been eradicated over the past two centuries to the point that they now numbered less than a tenth the population of the year 1803.

"Why 1803?" Marcy said. "Who knows how many Apaches there were then? We didn't exactly take censuses."

"Okay, okay," Buffalo Dong said. "Follow that story through. Did they get their political asylum?"

She flicked on to the next day and then the next.

Frank Barboncito and his companions were granted political asylum by a unanimous vote of the French Assembly. And the next day they'd gone to work. They demanded that the French Government declare the Louisiana Purchase invalid. The purchase had been made during the reign of Napoleon, who had seized power illegally during the coup d'état of the 18th Brumaire. The Louisiana Purchase was hence illegal and the whole area was in actuality still the property of the Republic of France. Moreover, the Apache Indians were loyal subjects of France, since at the time of the Louisiana Purchase they had lived in a part of America illegally ceded to the United States. The students demanded the Apaches be returned to their original tribal lands, which they had owned under the French and had never legally signed away.

"Holy Mackerel," March said. "Is that all the McCoy?"

"Partially, I think," Jim told her. "Some of the Apaches lived over on Louisiana Purchase country. See if you can get anything about Daisy and the kids down in Mexico."

Daisy Armijo and her four fellow Marijuaneros had appealed for the status of political refugees, citing the same claim as had the Apache students in France. They were afraid to return to the States and threw themselves on the mercy of the Mexican people. Their fellow students at the University of Guadalajara had hit the streets in their support. The Mexican Congress, never loath to take a backhanded swing at the gringos on the other side of the Rio Grande, had immediately ruled in their favor.

And the next day, the Apache refugees had demanded that the Mexican government appeal to the Reunited Nations for a return of parts of Texas, New Mexico, Arizona and California which had been stolen from them as a result of a war of aggression, which even Abraham Lincoln had condemned while still a Representative. The Apaches announced that they wished to be returned to a southwest once again under the sovereignty of Mexico, claiming that the Mexicans, while still in control, had never oppressed the Indians as did the white Americans as soon as they had taken over.

Hank looked at Buffalo Dong and said, "Gee, how does that jibe with us wanting the French to take back the Louisiana Purchase? We can't claim to want to live under both the Mexicans and French."

"I can see you've got a lot to learn about international

diplomacy,'' the chief told him. ''We can claim every goddam thing we want and let the Mexicans and French work
out an accommodation. They'll both bend over backwards to
seem like good guys to everybody else—and that means
making us fat and happy. Remember Egypt and India.''

There came another loud knock from the direction of the
kitchen door and Jim went to answer it.

Their captives came in bearing trays again, this time
with four gigantic steaks and fixings.

''Ugh. Wow!'' Hank muttered.

The four lit into the steaks with malicious intent, while
their captives stood back looking apprehensive but hopeful.

Still chewing hard, Buffalo Dong looked up at them and
said, ''Ugh. You can take white man's firewagon and go.
Drive um very slow. Maybe twenty miles an hour. Apache
braves everywhere, watching roads. Shoot-um up anybody
goes too fast. You relay message for us to Great White
Father. Tell him, Apache Council has ruled no towns in
New Mexico and Arizona will be considered open cities.
Apaches get-um everybody, everywhere.''

The senior citizen blanched. His wife looked at him,
still fearful. ''What does that mean, dear? What's an open
city?''

''A city that the enemy has agreed not to bomb, shell,
or attack in other manner.''

''You betchum.'' Hank said, leering through his war
paint. ''This time Apache goes on warpath and get-um all
double-face white men. We gottum secret weapons.''

''Secret weapons!'' the white man blurted.

''Ugh. You betchum.''

Jim said, ''Ugh. Me go rip out car phone, so they no
able to call until they get to first town.'' He started for the
door and the two quaking whites turned to follow him.

"Ugh," Marcy said. "One more thing you remember. Very important." Slowly she said, "Great Spirit says, life is but a fart in the voluminous drawers of time."

Buffalo Dong rolled his eyes upward in mute appeal.

The two prisoners stared at her for a moment, then turned and headed after Jim, on their way to freedom.

Chapter Thirteen

Max Cohn had rented a sports model hovercar at the Coronado Auto-Pool. He could have walked the distance to the Chutzpa soul-farm but deep down within he had dreams of inviting JoJo for a drive. A check on the National Data Banks Banking files had indicated that the Chutzpas had no vehicles of their own and seldom expended their pseudo-dollar credits on vehicles, aside from rented hovertrucks, most likely when required for hauling feed or produce. Like most of the extended families living on the soul-farms, they seemed to prefer to walk, or to ride horseback. It was one of the things that drove the citizens of Coronado up the wall, especially the younger element, all of whom dreamed of the day when they could afford a privately owned car. Meanwhile, they spent as much of their GAS as possible on hiring them. The American romance with the speedy vehicle was slow a-dying in Coronado.

In actuality, Max himself approved of the Auto-Pool, being no car fan. In the old days, for all practical purposes, everybody had his own car, no matter how low their standard of living. Some families had two or even three. Their diet might have been inadequate, their clothing and shelter inadequate, but they would keep themselves hooked on cars, no matter what. Max had read figures somewhere once, indicating that an unbelievable percentage of the average American's income had gone into such transportation. Counting original cost, interest on the loan, depreciation, insurance, repairs and tires, fuel, oil and lubricants, even such items as parking, the cost of driving a private car came to something like 50¢ a mile, or $5000 a year per car, if the average mileage per annum was 10,000 miles. Given three cars in a family, that was $15,000 a year, over two hundred and fifty dollars a week. Max shook his head. Where in the world had the average family gotten it?

On top of all, most cars spent approximately four-fifths of their life spans parked. Parked at night in the family garage, in the streets, or in a parking lot.

Hertz and Avis had been two of the pioneers of change. Slowly car rentals took over from private ownership. Why buy a car that spent most of its time parked? Why not rent one for only the period you actually wanted it? Phone for a car when you wished one from the nearest Auto-Pool; and when you were through with it, return it. Most of the roads in the country were automated these days, and your ordered vehicle delivered itself, and returned itself sans driver. There was another sizable advantage. You could hire the type and size car you wished. If you were alone or with one other person, you could dial for a small economical two-seater, possibly a sports car, if you were going for a spin. If there were four of you, you dialed a sedan; if there were six or so, complete with kids and picnic hampers, you chose a station wagon or even a mini-bus. Yes, you had available any type hovercar you wished, and weren't limited to a family sedan with seats for five but which was usually occupied by a single person.

It had become the largest single government monopoly. With the whole Auto-Pool project in its hands, the government could buy the cars involved literally millions at a time, with all of the savings that involved. It also meant that you could pick up your rental car at any Auto-Pool in the country and return it to any other. It further meant that repairs and maintenance were standardized and automation could be used to the utmost. A car never went out without maintenance, never went out with inadequate tires or punctured air cushions and was periodically given a complete overhaul.

Of course, there were those who still preferred their own private cars. But Max Cohn wasn't in the category and didn't particularly want to be. He was no hovercar buff.

The Chutzpa place was but a few miles out of town, and Max Cohn had no difficulty finding it. He pulled up, not far from the steps that led down into the central patio, and looked about. Given water—and the Chutzpas obviously had water, probably from wells—this part of New Mexico could bloom like a garden, a wood, a golf course fairway, a Nisei truck farm. It could and did. Max looked around appreciatively before approaching the dwelling. He was not unacquainted with the type of architecture. The underground building, thanks to Malcolm Wells, was spreading throughout the country. But he had seen few as attractive as this.

At the steps, there seemed no bell nor identity screen nor other means to announce his coming. He hesitated. Max Cohn was not an aggressive young man. He started down the steps by forcing himself to think of JoJo.

In the large patio onto which he emerged, he found two women; well, a woman and a girl. They were stretched out on wooden, handcrafted lawn furniture, taking in the midday sun. The matronly woman was in halter and shorts. The young blonde was in shorts, period. Max swallowed. He was not exactly a prude—not exactly. He knew that some of the extended families practiced complete nudity and he got the quick feeling that ordinarily this girl might too, except that the denim shorts protected her rounded bottom from the slats of the chair, which was unadorned by cushions. What had set him back was the unbelievable lushness of her mammary glands, so pink tipped that he suspected cosmetics.

They both looked up at his hesitant approach. The matron was sewing.

Max said, "Uh, Mrs. Chutzpa?"

She smiled in hospitable fashion. "They call me Blackie."

The girl smiled brightly at him and said, "I'm Alice."

Max cleared his throat again and said, "My name is Maximilian Cohn. I'm from the Guaranteed Annual Stipend Administration. Ms. JoJo suggested . . ." He let his sentence dribble away.

"Oh, yes," Blackie said, nodding comfortably. "She mentioned the nice young man she met in town."

Max's inclination was to beam at that victory, but he said, "Uh . . . is Ms. JoJo at home?"

Blackie said, "I saw her a little while ago." She looked at the girl. "Sweet Alice, could you look for her? Take a load off, Max.'' She indicated the chair which Sweet Alice vacated.

The blond was now on her feet; exquisite feet, quite perfect, and quite innocent of nail polish. She donated a coquettish smile and went into the house. Her breasts bounced enticingly when she walked; he did what he could to keep his eyes from bouncing with their rhythm and turned back to Blackie. Had his masculinity not already been committed. . . .

''Nice tits, eh?'' Blackie said placidly.

''Uh, what?'' Max croaked.

''JoJo says she won't be able to get GAS because of some red tape or other. She didn't seem to know what it was all about.''

Max was on firmer ground now. He leaned forward, his adam's apple bobbing sincerely, ''That's why I came out. We have to know at least one of her parents' names or, at least, where Ms. JoJo was born.''

''Oh, that's no problem,'' Blackie said in relief. ''Her mother's name was, let's see now, Martha, no Nora, or something like that.''

Max Cohn inwardly winced. He said cautiously, ''You wouldn't know where Ms. JoJo was born, would you?''

Blackie put down one corduroy shirt and took up another and hunted around in a tin box for the right button. ''Hell, yes,'' she said, with all the doting affection of a grandmother, which she was obviously not. ''The little dear was born in the East, somewhere. Isn't she the sweetest thing you ever met?''

''Well, yes. But where in the East? What city? And exactly when?''

Blackie started working on the button, complacently. ''Some girls, when they're really pretty and stacked and all, are real cunts so far as character is concerned. But I've met a good many who aren't that way. They don't have to be, perhaps. They're so attractive that everybody loves them and they don't have to be bitchy. Back in the old days, when they still had movies, some of the really top stars such as Sophia Loren, Loretta Young and Ingrid Bergman, were adored by everybody. I don't mean the jerk movie fanatics, the hell with them. I mean the people that worked with them, which is what counts. You know, not only the directors and producers and all, but the grips and the electricians and the extras. They were real people. They didn't have to be bastards. Well, the way I see it, that's the way JoJo is. She's as sweet as she is pretty, and she's the prettiest thing I've ever seen come down the damn pike. Did you ever notice what a cute ass she has? Not that she's conscious of it, or anything. It's just . . . well . . .'' Blackie bit the end off of the thread and searched around in her sewing again.

Max was gaping at her. Every inclination he had, deep down within, said, yes, yes, he had noted the cute ass, as Blackie put it, but it was absolutely beyond him and would always be. He would only see it for the rest of his life in his dreams.

He gulped and said, ''Where was she born?''

''Oh. Yes. Well, I don't think anybody knows. Martha, no, her name must have been Nora . . .''

''Ms. JoJo said Nora.''

''. . . yes, Nora. I don't believe she ever mentioned it to me. Where JoJo was born, I mean. Except somewhere in the East. You know, Boston or Baltimore, or somewhere. Although, come to think of it, Nora didn't seem the type to pad down in a city.''

Sweet Alice came back and since all the chairs were

taken, sank down on her back on the flagstones, her hands behind her head, throwing her most glorious features to the skies. She said, "Zack was in the saloon with Moon and Bitter Joe. He says JoJo's out in the apple orchard, pruning, or something, with the Professor and Ron. They oughta be back soon for lunch."

"That's nice," Blackie said. "Stop jiggling, dear, you're straining the young man's zipper. Besides, it's too early in the day for what you have in mind." She went back to Max. "Now, what was it you were saying? Oh, yes, Nora. Well, I'm afraid that Nora was something of a baroque."

"A baroque?"

"That's right. When I was a child, they called them beatniks, or beats, for the beat generation. Then when I was a girl they started calling them hippies, for the hip generation. Now they call them baroques, damned if I know why. There aren't so many anymore, most have joined up in extended families, or live on communes."

"But Nora, uh, JoJo's mother . . ."

Blackie thought about it, while adjusting her thimble. "Well," she said, "I guess for you to understand we'll have to go all the way back to how the family was formed. I was one of the first. So was Bitter Joe; he'd had one of his balls shot off during whatever war he was in. Not that it seemed to make much difference. He was a commie in those days, or a John Bircher or something like that, maybe a vegetarian. I was never able to tell the difference; they're all religions to true believers. Anyway, we had a fishing camp on the Saint Johns River, near Astor, in Florida. Pretty as a goddam picture there, with all the cypress and the live oaks and the hyacinths in the river and all."

Max was already tired of the lengthy development, but held his peace. JoJo would evidently be coming in shortly.

"People were always coming and going," Blackie said, her facial expression placid with the memory. "Usually, singles and doubles, sometimes people who said they were married, sometimes a single with a kid or two, sometimes a double or triple with kids, married or not. There weren't any rules. Anybody could get screwed anyway they damn well pleased."

She smiled reminiscently, in her motherly charm. "We thought of ourselves as a commune. Sometimes, if somebody got sick or some other expense came up, we'd find out that somebody in the commune had bread they could lay on us. That's what we said in those days. Bread meant money and lay on meant give us. It would embarrass a person to say, 'give me money,' but not to say 'lay some bread on me.' You can make the most outrageous demand if you do it in style. They'd send an emergency telegram to somebody, and the money'd come. We still had old-fashioned money in those days. Well, as time went by we got tougher and tougher about the baroques—like I said, we called them hippies in those days—they'd sponge on the rest of us who'd do the chores. Cook, clean up, do the fishing, do the hunting—we used to get a lot of squirrels and coot and ducks and sometimes a wild pig—or find the swamp cabbage . . ."

"Swamp cabbage?" Sweet Alice said, taking the opportunity to jiggle again.

"I told you to cut that out. You're distracting the poor boy," Blackie said mildly. "Swamp cabbage. Heart of palm. It'd cost you ten bucks or so a throw in a classy restaurant in New York or Paris. But we ate it every day. Got burnt-out on the damn stuff, to tell the truth."

Max said, with a touch of pleading: "All right, you

had a commune. How did the Chutzpa family ever get started? And Nora, and JoJo. . .''

"Like I said, we got tired of the baroques. We had to work, kind of. For cash money we'd fish for catfish. The St. Johns River was full of them. The crackers. . .''

"Crackers?" Sweet Alice said, refraining as ordered from jiggling.

"Florida crackers. The natives. They wouldn't touch what they called shit-eating catfish. But you could sell them for twenty-five cents a pound to be shipped up to St. Louis where folks were ape about catfish. The poor cubes up there—we used to call them squares in those days— thought they were fresh out of the Mississippi.''

Max cleared his throat apologetically. "The family. The Chutzpas.''

"Oh yes," Blackie said, taking up still another bit of sewing, a child's set of denims this time. "Well, we got more and more selective about who we let into the group, like. We used to say *like* in those days. If they didn't do their share, we'd have a confab and ask them to move on. Not tough, you know, but we asked them. Some got a little sore, but we figured, screw 'em. And as time went by, the ones that stayed on got more and more compatible—like. And more permanent. Some of us'd pair off and have a kid. And we got harder and harder about letting newcomers in. Not that anybody who was on their way through couldn't stay for as long as they wanted, if they did their share. But we didn't want anymore bad news types. And after awhile we had what they called a family, instead of a commune. And when GAS started, and we all signed up for it, somebody—I think Bitter Joe—came up with the name Chutzpa. . .''

"That can't be it," Max said sotto voce, but couldn't

bring himself to interrupt the long story by the nice, pleasantly graying woman.

". . . and we all had our name legally changed to that, and we opened our family account in the National Data Banks and from then on we had our family kitty."

"But, uh, Nora and JoJo."

"Oh, well, we decided what we wanted was a soul-farm, to raise our own food and all, so we moved out here and took up land. And we weren't here very long when Nora came with JoJo and was a real whiz at first and changed her name to Chutzpa, like the rest of us. But she got bored and moved on."

"But JoJo!"

"Oh, we all liked her and she liked us and the place and all, so she stayed."

"But her mother, uh, Nora. She just *left* her?"

Blackie frowned and thought about it whilst threading another needle. "I think she became a butch, or something. At any rate, she went off with another girl who was on her way through."

Max was on the verge of giving up, but couldn't. Certainly not until he had at least seen JoJo again. He couldn't believe she actually resembled the vision in his memory.

He said desperately, "But couldn't somebody else remember more about JoJo's parents?"

Blackie said vaguely, "You might try Bitter Joe. He's been with the family just about as long as I have."

Sweet Alice said helpfully, "He's in the saloon getting smashed with Moon. You want me to take you there, before I show you your room?"

He looked at her blankly. "What room?"

Sweet Alice said brightly, "Oh, I thought you'd stay for the night."

"Now you hush up, dear," Blackie said. "And take Max in to talk with Bitter Joe. Get him a nice cold glass of cider. We'll have lunch shortly—I think. Did the spirit move anybody to cook?"

Sweet Alice got to her feet with uncontrolled jiggling. She said, "I think Franny. She said something about broiling bass with a curry rubbed over it. Something she learned in Bombay."

Max had stood too, politely, in anticipation of going to meet more of this family. He couldn't refrain from saying, "Bombay? You mean. . . ?"

Sweet Alice said sweetly, "I think she went there with somebody she was laying that wanted to shoot a tiger, or something. Wasn't it a tiger, Blackie?"

"A kangaroo," Blackie said, thinking back. "As I recall, Franny said he wanted to shoot it with a bangerang. Boomerang? Oh, well—"

Max shuddered again, but obediently followed Sweet Alice to the saloon.

Chapter Fourteen

There were two men and a small dog in the large living room. At least, Max thought it looked something like a dog. The creature was up on a couch, probably sleeping. Of the two men, the older, glass in hand, was staring off into the distance. The younger, a black, was at a desk working on some notes with a stylo. He looked up when Sweet Alice entered with Max.

Sweet Alice said, "This is Maximilian Cohn, from Coronado. He's here to see JoJo about GAS."

Moon said, "Hi, Max. My name's Moon. I'm the newest addition to the Chutzpa family." He waved a hand gently, in lieu of getting up and shaking. Then he picked up a glass from the desk and took an appreciative swig.

But Bitter Joe turned in his chair and looked at the newcomer with unconcealed sour pleasure. "I'll be damned," he said. "Cohn, is it? I haven't met a kike in this part of the country for years."

Moon laughed and said, "Don't worry about Bitter Joe. He's against all religions and all races. He's against niggers too. Sit down, Max. Get you a drink?"

The dog said—Max was almost sure it was a dog—"The bastard probably hates mutts too. If I had the energy, I'd fang him on the ankle."

Max sank into a chair. These people were continually confusing him. He could have sworn he'd heard spoken sarcasm from that ball of dirty black hair on the couch.

"I'll get you a cider," Sweet Alice said, with an enticing flick of her fanny as she turned toward the little bar.

"I'm not against religion," Bitter Joe said. "It's a great idea. The trouble is, most of the people who have been active in dreaming it up have had damn little imagination. Now take the Jewish, Christian, Moslem conception of God—they've all got the same one, of course. I've seen photographs of Him portrayed on the ceiling of the Sistine Chapel. He created man in His own image. One hell of a lot of gods do. The Greek gods, for instance. They created man so similar to themselves that they could go around fighting each other, in the Trojan War and such, and screwing each other. Half of the big heroes and kings in ancient Mediterranean times were crosses between gods and humans. The Romans carried it on, after the Greeks. Julius Caesar was supposedly descended from the god Mars. But anyway, God, according to His portrait done by Mike Angelo in the Sistine Chapel, was an old duffer about seventy or so with a long white beard. It took Him five days of puttering to create the world but only one day to create the sun and all of the rest of the universe. Not just our galaxy, mind you, but all of the galaxies. I understand that there's at least billions of them, and ours is kind of small. But that didn't faze God, and why should it? But now He notes each sparrow that falls, and any-where else the equivalent happens, anywhere and all the time. But what I'm asking is this, the old question. What in the hell did He do with Himself before He created the galaxy? In all the infinity of time, what did He *do* to stave off boredom? I can see that He might have got a lot of laughs, there on top of Mt. Sinai with Moses, laying down the rules for the kikes, and telling them that they had to cut the skin off their dongs or He'd be all upset. But what the hell did He do for kicks before He dreamed up the uni-verse for a practical joke?''

Max had suffered through this tirade, eyes wide.

Sweet Alice brought him a tall glass of something cold and handed it over and then went to Moon's desk to see if he wanted a refill.

Moon said to her, ''Fair warning, Sweet Alice: If you stick one of those things in my eye, I'm going to bite it.''

Zack came into the room, spotted the newcomer and said, ''Hi. I'm Zack. You're the guy who works for the government on GAS, eh?'' He headed for the bar.

Bitter Joe said, ''Oh, you work for the government, eh? One of the most reactionary governments the world's ever seen. Hypocrites, too. The way they're always talking about American liberty and freedom, you'd think we were so free we'd all take off and drift away.''

''I . . . uh,'' Max said. ''How do you mean?'' He took a sip of the drink he held and then looked down into the glass reproachfully. It tasted something like apple juice with an erection. Max wasn't much of a drinking man.

Bitter Joe waved his own glass a little, as though in explanation. ''The last advanced country in the world to abolish slavery. And the last to declare equal rights for women. The last advanced country in the world to establish some sort of subsidized medical care so that even the poor could receive good medical attention.''

Max sat there and looked unhappy.

The dog said, ''He doesn't like Americans either.''

This time, Max couldn't keep himself from staring at the animal. He knew damned well the thing had talked.

Moon said, as though it explained everything, ''That's Bowser.''

Zack added as he returned to the rest, glass in hand, ''He's a Sazarac,'' as though that explained anything else that needed explaining.

Max took a long pull at his apple juice, though it had more—more chutzpa!—than he would have preferred. He knew he had to say something. He said to Bitter Joe, ''Then you're not proud to be an American?''

''Why should I be?'' Bitter Joe said sourly. ''I had nothing to do with it. By pure chance, I happened to be born in the United States. I didn't ask to be. It just happened that my parents were Americans. I suppose that if I'd been born in Japan, or Lapland, or the Congo, people would expect me to be proud of being a Jap, a Lapp, or a Congolese pygmy.''

Bitter Joe was just getting stoked up. He said, ''When I was a kid, we Americans had a pathetic assurance that we had the highest standard of living in the world. That we had the highest per capita incomes, that we ate the best food and were housed the best. We not only believed it, we *knew* it. It was a faith. Actually, the highest per capita income was in some of the Arab oil countries. The highest standards of living were in the Scandinavian countries and Switzerland. There were no such things as slums in those nations, no hungry people such as we had in Appalachia, the rural South and some Indian reservations, no such thing as inadequate medical and dental care. We were far down the list in life expectancy, and our diet had more junk food in it than the rest of the world even knew about. To tell a visiting European that American food was the best in the world was to invite the gag response.''

Max said desperately, ''Well, actually, I came here on government business. I'm the local head, well, actually, I'm the only employee of the GAS Administration in the Coronado area. As I understand it, all of you members of the Chutzpa, uh, family are on, GAS, and—''

Zack interrupted, to refute that. ''Not quite all. Colleen works in town in the administration of the Ultra-Market. And I'm going to drop off GAS too as soon as I come up with some novelty idea that'll put the whole family on easy street.''

''Ha,'' Sweet Alice said. She was the only one who hadn't a glass in hand. Her expression indicated that she was vacant enough without needing booze.

Zack glared at her. ''Oh, yes I am,'' he said. ''If I haven't come up with my fad, or whatever, before the year is out, I'll eat your hat, box and all.''

Max flinched at that.

Bowser muttered, ''Could I watch?''

Bitter Joe said, as though to soothe the younger member of the family, ''What's the latest project, Zack?''

And, truly enough, Zack was mollified. ''Well, golly, I'm working on an adaptation of the bullwhip. Something the man, or kid, in the street can get the hang of with just a few hours of practice.''

''Bullwhip?'' Moon said.

''Yeah, yeah.'' Zack waxed enthusiastic. ''Like the gauchos used to use down on the pampas in Argentina. They got to the point where they could take a bullwhip and put an apple on somebody's head and peel and quarter it from twenty or thirty feet. You know, just snapping the whip.''

"Oh, boy," Sweet Alice said.

"Well, how are you doing on it?" Bitter Joe said, trying to keep skepticism from his voice.

"I'm practicing, but it's not easy to get the hang of it," Zack said, making an unhappy face, which, in view of the fact that his face wasn't overly happy to begin with, didn't add to his photogenic qualities. "Besides, the damn things are too big to carry around. Zorro used to. . ."

"Zorro?" somebody said.

"Yeah," Zack nodded. "You know, in the old old movie revivals. Douglas Fairbanks. *Zorro* and *The Mark of Zorro* and the *Son of Zorro*."

"All right, all right," Moon said. "And all the rest, I suppose. What did Zorro do with his bullwhip?"

"He used to wrap it around his stomach. Then, when the baddies would come along he'd real quick rip open his shirt and. . ."

They were all leveling their eyes on him.

He coughed uncomfortably. "Well, that's the trouble. They're too big to be carried around. And it sure takes a lot of practice to get onto a bullwhip."

The door to the kitchen pushed open and Franny came in, wiping her hands briskly on an apron. She immediately recognized Max as the sole Posterity Party member in Coronado, but said nothing. He blinked surprise but had enough self-possession left to make no indication of their earlier meeting.

Moon made introductions and she smiled at the newcomer and shook hands. She said, "Somebody said something about JoJo having trouble getting her GAS." She headed over for the bar, taking Max's almost empty glass with her.

"I . . . I don't think I'll have any more," he protested.

"Oh?" her eyebrows went up. "Doc won't like you. He's proud of his spiked hard cider. But I'll get you something better."

He was about to protest that, but decided that she meant a soft drink and he could use it to chase down the potent potable he had just finished.

However, she returned with a pair of three-ounce glasses, each filled with a suspicious golden liquid.

"I'll put on another curried bass for lunch," she said, and thrust one glass at Max. "You're staying, of course?"

"Why, thanks." It meant that he'd be seeing that much more of JoJo, when she returned from the orchard.

Franny said, "Well, down the hatch," and knocked back the contents of her glass.

Obviously, it couldn't be as strong as all that, the unsophisticated Max decided. He followed suit.

And then realized, his eyes popping, that he'd made a great mistake. It *could* be as strong as all that, and was. He felt as though it would take very little effort to spit out his teeth.

The dog said, in his squeaky voice, "Tastes like mother's milk, eh?"

"Shut up, Bowser," Moon told him.

Franny, not noticing the guest's distress, said, "What's wrong with JoJo's application?"

Max swallowed twice and got out, "We can't seem to locate either her mother or father, or where she was born."

Franny said, "Oh?" She looked thoughtful, went over to the bar and, to Max's horror, poured herself another slug of the liquid dynamite, as big as the first, and tossed it back as though it were fruit juice. "That shouldn't be too difficult. I heard from Nora a couple of years ago."

Bitter Joe said, finishing his own drink. "You did? I didn't know that. Where was she?"

"In some commune or other up in the Catskill Mountains. She had used up all of her month's GAS and located me, somehow, and wanted a loan. I transferred some pseudo-dollars to her account."

"She always was a freeloader," Bitter Joe said. "Did she ever pay it back?"

"I don't believe so," she said absently and looked at Max. "I don't remember just where in the Catskills she was, but that shouldn't be too difficult to track down—if she's still there."

"Possibly not," Max said. "And if, ah, Nora is on GAS it would indicate that she's an American citizen in which case, Ms. JoJo would be too."

It was then that JoJo entered from the patio. She entered gaily, happily, freshly. It was obvious she had been joking with the two men who followed.

Max stumbled quickly to his feet and viewed her.

Behold, thou art fair, my love; behold thou art fair; thou hast doves' eyes within thy locks: thy hair is as a flock of goats, that appear from the mount of Gilead. Thy lips are like a thread of scarlet, and thy speech is comely; thy temples are like a piece of pomegranate within thy locks.

JoJo said, "Why, it's Mr. Cohn from Coronado. How nice."

Max knew, vaguely, that he was being introduced to the Professor and Ron. But he didn't hear. He allowed his hand to be shaken, but his eyes were all for JoJo.

He didn't even hear the dog say, more or less under its breath, "Jesus, love at first sight."

JoJo was saying, a slight distress in her voice, "Why, these unhospitable wretches haven't even offered you a drink. Sit down, Mr. Cohn. Couldn't I get you a drink?"

"Uh . . . oh, sure. Thanks," Max fumbled out. It was worse than it had been in town. He was all but tongue-tied.

JoJo was back in a moment with another of the long, cool hard ciders and—charmingly, he thought—extended it to him. "Now you sit down and be comfortable."

Max obeyed orders and sank back into his seat. Nervously, he drank the full contents of the glass, in desperate attempt to indicate how much he appreciated anything from her soft hand.

It was a mistake, and already he could begin to feel a sly fog rolling in over his mind.

Lunch didn't help much. Other members of the family drifted into the saloon; other introductions were made and promptly forgotten by Max Cohn. Nor was he following the trend of conversation any too well. The difficulty with lunch was that one of the family, a chubby one named Doc, insisted that Franny's superlative bass be washed down with a kind of beer he home-brewed from corn.

After the meal, when all were relaxing for digestive purposes, the apricot and peach brandy were brought forth. Max began to despair that the whole Chutzpa family was composed of dipsomaniacs. However, his snifter glass came from the hands of JoJo herself and he couldn't bear refusing.

There was some speculation on getting in touch with JoJo's mother, but he didn't follow it very well. As disconcerting as anything else was the fact that the dog seemed to enter periodically into the conversation. Max knew perfectly well that this must be his imagination; nevertheless the impression continued. Nobody else seemed to notice it. He could even have sworn that the animal had a somewhat wry sense of humor.

He had no idea how long he sat there, that late afternoon and early evening, grinning inanely, and not allowing himself to talk. He vaguely recalled someone insisting that he try Doc's sparkling cider, which was claimed to be so like champagne that you couldn't tell the difference. He couldn't remember if he complied or not.

From a great distance, he seemed to hear Blackie say in sympathy, "Why, the poor sonofabitch is drunk."

And from a greater distance still came the voice of Moon, saying, "He can't be very drunk; I just saw him move."

When Max awakened in the morning, it was in a strange bed. He was dying. He knew why his mother had always told him that good Jewish boys were always moderate drinkers. What she meant by moderation was a single glass of thick, sweet kosher red wine, on religious holidays. His memory, his head, his roiling stomach, the taste in his mouth, all told him that he had put away enough to have floated the ark, and it hadn't been kosher wine.

He opened his eyes experimentally, with little or no desire to continue the experiment unless miraculously encouraged.

The miracle occured.

And his eyes popped.

On the pillow next to his was a superb thatch of jet black hair, crowning a sympathetic and smiling face.

"Good morning, Max," JoJo said. "How are you feeling?"

Chapter Fifteen

John Shay eyed the metropolis of Coronado without joy.

City born and bred, he had never been in a town this size for longer than overnight, and only then as a rest stop while driving across country. And of all the few small towns he had stopped in he couldn't remember one more drab than this. Every old cliche he'd ever heard about small towns applied, from the suggestion that they rolled the streets up at night, to the one about watching haircuts for excitement.

He wasn't even sure why he had been dispatched to this outpost. Supposedly, Francesca de Rudder, one of the rip-snorting rocket-set broads, might be running interference for Shay's underground radical target, Ross Prager. She had last used her credit card here. Which didn't mean much, of course. By this time she could be half a continent away. He couldn't imagine a rocket-set member being found dead in a place like Coronado. But his instructions were to remain here until he heard further from Director Roy Thomas.

He had arrived the night before and had taken a motel room on the outskirts of town. He'd gone through Coronado first and found that his only alternative was a small hotel, right off the town's plaza. He had driven around the block a couple of times but didn't like anything about the hotel, including its appearance and probable lack of comfort. But, above all, it didn't look very promising so far as a quick hit was concerned. If he had to leave town in a hurry, he didn't want to go through the rigamarole of getting his hovercar out of a garage, nor driving through streets with which he wasn't acquainted.

No. The motel was his best bet, crummy though it was.

The following morning, he drove the half mile into town and had breakfast at the Auto-Cafeteria, sitting almost alone in the sterile dining room, dialing an uninspiring meal and paying for it by putting his credit card in the payment slot.

John Shay had heard that the one thing they couldn't louse up in the worst of restaurants was bacon and eggs, toast and coffee. Whoever had said that had been wrong.

He walked around the town a little, begrudging the stares of the locals, who evidently were not accustomed to strangers. There was an automated movie house. There were three bars, two of them automated. There was an Ultra-Market at which he could have purchased a bottle, but John Shay was not a drinking man. He couldn't afford to drink in his line of work.

Blue Jazus! Suppose that old fart Thomas kept him in this town for a month.

He went back to the motel and looked at the Tri-Di for awhile. The news was fifty-fifty about the Apaches and the

Second Constitutional Convention, neither of which held any interest for him.

He dialed the National Data Bank's Entertainment Section and located an ancient James Cagney movie. He watched it through to the bitter end, occasionally snorting contempt. In Shay's experienced view, Cagney was roughly as convincing a gunman as John Shay would have been as a matinee idol.

Like a good many not accustomed to reading, he had the ability to sleep when there was nothing else to do. It was hardly more than noon, but he took a nap.

He awoke at dusk. Shay considered getting in touch with the Division of Clandestine Services, but decided the hell with it. He was carrying his cloak and dagger communicator about with him—it looked like a wristwatch, and was, but was also more—and if they had anything to tell him, they would.

He could have walked back into town, but didn't. He had no desire to get more than a few yards away from his vehicle at any given time. He drove in and parked before the town's one bar which boasted a bartender. Its name was *El Last Chance*, and he snorted inwardly at that. Its external decor was a sad attempt at duplicating a saloon of the Old West.

The interior of *El Last Chance* looked like every other bar down through the ages. Somehow, if you've seen one you've seen them all—probably since the days of Omar Khayyám. John Shay stepped in and then to one side of the door and looked about, taking his time to let his eyes adjust to the dimness. There were only four others present; a man and woman in a booth, looking as though they were more interested in conversation than the glasses of beer before them; a white-aproned bartender; and a customer on a stool talking with the bartender. Evidently, it was too early for the rush hour—if there was ever a rush hour in Coronado. Only the bartender looked up at Shay's entrance.

John Shay went down to the end of the bar and took a stool from which he could see the door. He had never heard of Wild Bill Hickok but he knew enough to sit with his back to a wall when in a public place.

The bartender moved the short distance to Shay and said, "What'll it be, stranger?"

The city man's sole reason for being in *El Last Chance* was that he wanted to get the feel of the town. There wasn't much else he could accomplish until he heard from the Director. And you never knew; you just might pick up something that would be of use later on. Shay looked at the meager selection of bottles behind the bar. He had never seen such a limited display.

He said, "What've you got?"

"Muscatel, tequila, whiskey and the coldest beer in the West."

"What kind of whiskey?"

"Old Battle Fatigue."

"I'll have a whiskey and water."

The bartender put his two hands on the edge of the bar and said evenly, "We don't serve no fancy mixed drinks here."

John Shay looked at him for a long empty moment. He said finally, "Let me have a beer."

The bartender brought forth a glass, considered it for a moment, wiped it inside and out with his dirty apron, and put it on the bar. He reached down below again and came up with a plastic of beer, popped it open, poured it into the glass and pushed it before the newcomer.

"Coldest in the West," he said. "Drink hearty."

John Shay didn't touch it for the time being and the bartender, resuming his leaning stance, said hospitably, "Where you from, stranger? We don't see many tourists in these here parts."

"The East," Shay said. He was here to strike up a conversation so he added, in the way of taking the edge off the curtness, "On my way through to the coast, and I kind of like it here." He thought for a moment, trying to come up with something that a sane man might like about Coronado. "The mountains and the high altitude air, and all."

The other man at the bar, two stools down, said glumly, "And all what? If I could raise enough pseudo-dollar credit to get out of this flea-trap town, I'd been gone a coon's age ago."

The bartender said, "Hell, Paco, if you didn't drink up your monthly GAS two weeks after it's credited to your account, you'd have enough to light out."

John Shay said, "At any rate, I thought I might stay over a few days. Kind of rest up. I'm in no hurry. Don't have to be in San Diego for quite awhile." He'd dropped that on purpose, knowing it'd filter through town before the next day was out. He didn't want people to start wondering why he was hanging around.

Paco looked over at Shay. "You driving through to the coast? Aren't you afraid of the Indians?"

Shay sipped at his beer, or pretended to. "How do you mean?" he said.

The other got down from his stool, glass in hand, and moved down to the one next to the visitor.

"The Apaches, the Apaches," he said. "Everybody's clearing out. All northern New Mexico, most of Arizona, lots of people in southern Colorado. Everything's jammed.

Airlines, rocket shuttles, monorails, not to say nothin' about the roads. Raton Pass is so jammed up with cars and trucks and buses, they won't clear it out for months. People just gave up finally and let their cars and trucks just sit there on the road for something like fifty miles. The army can't get through. They're calling up military bulldozers to shove 'em off the road. Figure they'll destroy a hundred million pseduo-dollars worth of vehicles.''

"What army?'' the bartender said. "I didn't listen to no news today.''

"The regular army's ordered in two armored divisions,'' Paco said with satisfaction. "Going to clean out this Buffalo Dong and his warriors once and for all. General Peterflogger is mad as a wet piss-ant. He wanted all the credit for hisself and the National Guard.''

The bartender said, "I heard all the insurance companies were going broke in the whole Southwest, on account of everybody leaving. Just deserting their homes and businesses. Looters everywhere. Fires breaking out every which way and nobody to take care of putting them out. Crops all going to hell. Nobody to supervise the automated agricultural machines. Everything's going to pot.''

"Yeah,'' Paco said. "And those damn Indians that went to the Reunited Nations. They're causing one shit of a stink. They've got the Russians swung over to supporting them.''

"The Russians?'' Shay said. "What the hell have they got to do with it?''

"Well, this here Apache who leads the Indian delegation, seems he took his lawyer training at Harvard. He comes up with the claim the Indians are all Russians.''

Both Shay and the bartender looked at him blankly.

The other had the limelight and obviously liked it. He

said importantly, "What he says is, all the Indians came over from Siberia, by the Bering Straits. Siberia is Russian. So the Indians are Russians and they're making a big plea for the Soviets to back them. And acourse, the Russians love any chance to get a knee in old Uncle Sam's groin. So they're putting up a howl that the United States give in to the Marijuaneros."

Shay said, "Look, how come you people here in Coronado aren't clearing out? I heard on a news broadcast those Apaches have laser assault rifles. You know what the hell they are? One Apache with one of those guns could cut this whole town down in two minutes flat."

The bartender shook his head and snorted. "Nahhh. We get along all right with the Indians. Hell, we're mostly Indians ourselves. Us folks were living right here in Coronado hundreds of years before there ever was any United States. They call us Spanish-Americans, but we're mostly Indians, Mexicans, and just a little Spanish, all mixed up."

In actuality, John Shay didn't give a damn about the Indians. He figured that he could hold his own. He changed the subject. "What else is in the news?"

Paco made circular motions over his glass to indicate his desire for another drink and the bartender reached for the tequila bottle and poured.

Paco said, "Nothing but that damned Second Constitutional Convention. You know, it gets more and more clear that all those politicians are a bunch of crooks. They're every one out for themselves. It was never so clear before. But now they're all out to change the laws and all, you can see it plain as day. Stupid bastards to begin with and all out for themselves. They don't give a popcorn fart about the country. None of them. It's too bad a bunch of these

Posterity Party guys aren't there. They're the only ones that aren't crooks."

Shay's ears pricked up at that last, but his face remained expressionless.

"What're you talking about in particular?" the bartender said, resuming his leaning stance against the bar.

"Ah," Paco said. "This thing today. The Labor Party."

"That's a new one," the bartender said.

"They've got a couple dozen of them, these small parties, these days. Each one out for himself and the hell with the country. This here Labor Party wants the new constitution to have a House of Labor, instead of a House of Representatives. They say everything produced comes from Labor, so labor ought to run the country."

"I never even heard of them," the bartender protested. "Who the hell does any labor any more? You can't get a laborer's job in industry; it's all automated."

"Well, the way I get it, they're leftover from when there was unions. The more automation came in, the more the union workers dropped off. After awhile, there was nobody left in the unions but these labor leaders and their goons and a helluva lot of them was Mafia. You know how bad money drives out good? Well—same goes for management. Labor unions was one of the biggest rackets in the country. As soon as the government took over with the computers selecting the best guy suitable for whatever jobs were left, union members dropped out like dandruff. There wasn't nothin' in it for them."

John Shay was scowling. "Then how come all these unions didn't just fold up?"

The other was triumphant in his knowledge. "Because they had these big strike funds, and pension funds and the union treasury and all. So these bigwig union leaders and their goons just sat round and elected each other to office and voted each other big salaries from the interest on all the money they controlled. And no laws broke, see?''

''What a racket,'' Shay said in honest admiration. ''I've never heard of it. I don't suppose they'd go in much for publicity, though. But what's all this about their Labor Party?''

''I guess nobody's ever satisfied,'' the other said. ''I guess they didn't have much to do with their time, so they started the Labor Party and now they wanta get their foot in the door of the government and *really* get on the gravy train.''

John Shay's wristwatch buzzed softly. He looked down at it in surprise. He wasn't used to the thing as yet.

''What the hell's that?'' the bartender said, scowling.

''Oh,'' Shay said, flicking the stud in. ''Alarm. I got something I have to do. Where's the john?''

The bartender pointed it out and Shay went over and locked the door behind him before bringing the wrist device to his face and saying, after activating it, ''Shay. What spins?''

A tinny voice said, ''Are you where you can talk—and listen? There's quite a bit.''

John Shay said, ''Well, no. I'll go back to my cabin and call you back.''

He went back into the barroom and headed for the door.

''Hey,'' the bartender called. ''You didn't drink your beer.''

''Not cold enough,'' Shay said, and left.

He drove back to the motel, parked and went in. He went about the room, checking the two windows to be sure they were closed, locked the door and then sat down to the small desk. He unsnapped the wristwatch and propped it up on the desk, activated it, leaned closer and said, "Shay here."

A tiny voice said, "One moment, please," and then, a moment later, a voice, despite its smallness, that could be recognized as that of Director Roy Thomas came through.

"Shay?"

"That's right."

"Very well. We've had a break. We don't know why, but possibly this Ross Prager has a sense of humor. He's made a mistake with the false identity he took. To this point he hadn't used the Universal Credit Card. Hadn't bought a thing, so we couldn't get a fix on him. Then, out of a clear sky, several thousands of pseudo-dollar credit got transferred to his account. What happened, we don't know, but only a few hours later, it was transferred back again to the account from which he had derived it."

"From who?" Shay said flatly, "And where?"

"Right there in Coronado. From the account of the Chutzpa family."

"Chutzpa family?" the hit man said blankly. "Isn't that a Jew word meaning . . ."

"Yes," the other said impatiently. "But the hell with that. We've been checking them out every way possible. It's one of these so-called extended families. They're all over the country, these days. The thing we turned up is this. Francesca de Rudder is kind of a member of this family."

"Kind of?"

"Correct. She's been with them, off and on, for over fifteen years. Why, God only knows. Probably some silly way of getting her kicks. At any rate, she turns up at their place every six months or so and stays for awhile. We suspect that she's taken Prager there, figuring it's a good place for him to hide out. Who in the hell would figure on him going to ground in a crackpot commune?''

"You think he's there now?'' Shay said, his hunter instinct tingling in his veins.

"Perhaps. From what we understand, this Chutzpa family is really far gone. They don't draw any color line or . . .''

"Color line? What in the hell's that got to do with it?''

There was a momentary pause. Then the Director said, "Didn't I tell you Prager was a Black?''

"You mean this guy's a dinge? Blue jazus, I thought he was the big brain writing all this dangerous crap.''

The Director said, impatiently, "We haven't got any time to go into that. The Egyptians were Africans, you know. They had a pretty big civilization when your ancestors were running around in animal skins.''

John Shay was neither anthropologist nor historian. He said, "Okay, okay. What do I do now? Play it by ear? Just bust in and start shooting, or what?''

The small voice in the instrument said, "Goddammit, don't even joke about it! I told you, this is the most hush-hush assignment you've ever had. If at all possible, it has to look like an accident. There can be nothing that gets into the news media. You were recommended to us without reservation. Your specialty is making a, ah, hit look like an accident. That's what we want. This must not get to the media. Things are becoming chaotic. Convening this Second Constitutional Convention was a fantastic mistake. It's revealing to the whole country how fouled up things have become. We of the elite . . .''

"Who in the hell's the elite?'' Shay growled.

"Never mind. This is an upper echelon matter that you wouldn't understand.''

"I'm not stupid.''

"Listen, your job is to get Prager, nothing else. In return, you'll live like the rocket-set for the rest of your life. But this is the thing: if Prager comes out with a new inflammatory pamphlet now, we've had it. The computers say . . . well, that's not important to you."

"What do the computers say?"

"Never mind, damn it."

"All right. How do I get in to make a hit that looks like an accident? I can't just be strolling by on a nice sunny day. If he's gone into hiding with these crackpots, they're covering for him. I couldn't even get through the door."

"We've got a cover for you. As I told you, we've checked this Chutzpa family out as thoroughly as possible. Everything in the data banks. Now then, they had a former member who still retains the name Nora Chutzpa. She hasn't lived with them for years. She's now living on a commune in upstate New York. She's evidently still more or less in communication with them since the National Data Bank records that Francesca de Rudder transferred some pseudo-dollars credit to her two years ago. We are not sure of this, but it would seem that she has a daughter still living with the family there in New Mexico. These people conduct themselves like idiots; there is practically no information on their private lives in the data banks. At any rate, this is your cover. We will transmit to you, over your regular phone screen . . . you have one in your cabin?"

"That's right."

"Very well. We'll transmit her complete dossier. Study it. Completely familiarize yourself with everything about her. Physical appearance, everything. Then go out to the Chutzpa place. They evidently live on one of these so-called soul-farms, a couple of hundred acres or so. Tell them you're a friend of Nora Chutzpa's on the way through and she suggested that you drop by and say hello. All very friendly, understand?''

"That's right."

"Very well. *Then* you start playing it by ear."

"How do I know this Ross Prager bastard when I see him, if he's going under a different name? Oh, yeah. He's a nigger.''

Chapter Sixteen

The four of them were stretched out on a ridge topped largely by cactus, sagebrush and stunted mesquite. None of them looked pleased. Buffalo Dong had his binoculars trained on the scene below.

Hank said unhappily, "We ought to drag ass out of here. This country's swarming."

Buffalo Dong growled, "Which is exactly why we can't get out until night. Some of the damn fools have taken to the open country, trying to get by the traffic jams. It would be just our luck to run into a scared bunch of them armed with sporting rifles, shotguns, God knows what. Oh, oh. Look what's coming."

The other three directed their eyes to where he was indicating. The scene below involved a river—small at this time of the year, the dry season—crossed by a high concrete bridge. The highway was an old, unautomated, two-lane affair, and probably usually didn't suffer more than a

single vehicle an hour. Now it was packed or, at least, the
aprons of the road were. Within view must have been at
least a thousand cars, both hover models and the old-
fashioned four-wheeled types, plus buses, campers, trailers,
motor hover-bikes and even a few old-fashioned foot-
powered bicycles. Around each vehicle was its contingent
of occupants. Some were standing, usually glaring at the
bridge, some were inside to escape the sun, especially
those who rejoiced in air conditioning. Some were seated
around, more or less in circles, in camping chairs or on the
ground. Some of these were making coffee over campfires
or camping stoves.

"Cripes," Jim muttered. "Where do they all come
from?"

Buffalo Dong growled, "You take the whole population
of a state and put them on the highway at once and things
like this happen, particularly when the damned fool Air
Force has blown down a few dozen major bridges, trying to
keep us from escaping this supposed entrapment." He
sniffed scorn. "But look at this coming."

The reason for the jam below was that military combat
police had taken over the road. Squads of them were
posted at each end of the bridge. Others were patrolling
up and down the highway itself, preventing any of the
civilian vehicles from getting up it.

And now the others could see what their chief was
referring to. Down the road, from the northeast, were
coming three monstrous battle tanks. The only members of
the tank crews visible were the commanders, their heads
and shoulders protruding above the hatches. Each major
turret gun was directed ahead but the smaller ones, mounted
at the sides, were continually tracking to each flank, as
though momentarily expecting to go into action.

Buffalo Dong snorted again. He muttered, ''Those stupid rumors on the news broadcasts that we'd captured some antitank guns have evidently got through to them.''

The lead tank came to the edge of the bridge and hesitated for a moment. The four Apaches could make out the tank commander, looking up and down the narrow stream, as though suspicious of a trap. The thousands of civilians, blocked by the military traffic, didn't seem to reassure him. Some of these were shouting in his direction, probably curses, though they couldn't be heard at this distance.

The commander evidently came to some conclusion since the heavy war juggernaut began to grind forward onto the bridge. The second tank advanced and came to a halt at the point from which the first had just left, and the third brought up the rear.

When the first tank reached the middle of the structure, they began to make their mistake. The second tank started forward.

''Damn fool,'' Buffalo Dong muttered, his eyes glued to his glasses.

''Why?'' Marcy said.

But her question was already answered. When the first tank had all but reached the far end of the bridge, and the second was in the middle, the third began to follow.

On the face of it, whatever contractor had been involved in the construction had picked up a few extra pseudo-dollars in conserving on the quality and amount of the cement. The bridge sighed mightily and in considerable dignity; then, amid tremendous dust and noise, crumbled to the bed of the stream below. The first tank had almost made it and for a moment its treads scrabbled desperately for the safety of the far bank. Then it too succumbed and, only a few moments later, joined its companions below.

Hank made the most inadequate of statements. "Gee," he said.

For awhile, the three tanks snorted and squirmed in the mass of concrete and steel reinforcing, and in the piling up of water and mud of the now temporarily damned river. And then, before they could be swamped, the crews poured from the hatches and desperately made good their escapes to the stream banks.

"Cripes," Jim said. "Another bridge down. How in the hell are all those people going to get to wherever they're going? This was already a detour for them."

Hank said, "Marcy, what's life?"

"An odorous turd in the bottomless cesspool of time," she told him.

"Thank God I now know."

"Okay, okay," Buffalo Dong said, putting away his binoculars in his pouch and then his glasses into a shirt pocket. "Let's take a chance and split. A bunch of these people are going to abandon their cars and take to their feet. It'd be just our luck for some of them to flush us."

They slithered backwards from their vantage point, then came to their feet and, crouched low, followed their war chief who led them deviously for a half mile before coming to a stop.

Jim was looking up into the skies. At various points, here and there, were aircraft, though none immediately overhead. Some, however, in the fairly near vicinity were slow moving helio-jets, making wide circles.

Jim said uncomfortably, "Aren't they supposed to have animal heat detectors? Be able to pick up our location with infra-red sensors."

"Yeah," Buffalo Dong said. "But with several thousand so-called refugees around, how are they going to tell the good guys from us bloodthirsty redmen?" He looked about and added, "Let's get in here for the time being."

"In here" was a ledge leaning over the goat path they had been following. It wasn't quite a cave but provided shelter as much as ten feet back. The four hustled into it. They couldn't have been seen from above.

The chief said, "Marcy, you're the commissary. What in the hell've we got left to eat?"

She fiddled in her pouch. "Six candy bars," she said. "The last from that stuff we liberated at the mountain lodge. We're going to have to do some more scrounging."

"Oh, yeah?" Hank said, fishing into his own pouch for the tiny transistor radio. "Well, according to the last news broadcast, General of the Armies Gunther 'Kill 'em All' Phartschmeller, who's now commander of the two Army Corps they've sent into the Southwest, has declared that all women combatants will be dealt with the same as males. Civilians under arms, male or female, will be considered irregulars and shot out of hand. And all Apaches are considered civilians; they don't recognize our belligerency status. At least we'll have women's lib hitting the ceiling over that one. However, you, as well as we, Marcy, are going to have to take it easy on scrounging."

"Maybe we'll run into some deserted homes with food still in them," Buffalo Dong said. "What was that about two Army Corps? I thought it was two armored divisions."

"They've upped it," Hank said, erecting the antenna from his small radio set. "Two Army Corps now."

Buffalo Dong shook his head. "What people," he said. "They would have been better off leaving it to the State Police. At least they know the country a little. Well, we

don't have those damned vigilantes cluttering up the woods
anymore.''

Jim's tone was contemptuous. "No," he said. "The
silly bastards shot so many of themselves by mistake that
they finally called it quits. Besides, when all the rumors
started flying about how we were out for gore, most of
them had second thoughts and split with their families for
Texas or California.''

Marcy handed out a candy bar to each. "We've got to
get some water, too," she said.

"After it gets dark," Buffalo Dong told her. "We can
go back to the stream and fill our canteens—if all those
people down there haven't drunk it dry. What's on the
news, Hank?''

Hank had been fiddling with the dials of the set.

There was plenty on the news.

"Hey," he said. "Hector and our other Rhodes scholars
at Oxford are causing a real stink in England. They got the
political asylum they asked for yesterday and now they're
badgering the Queen.''

"What about?" Marcy said wearily. She was too far
from the set to hear its small volume. "What in the devil's
the Queen got to do with it? If she lasts much longer she'll
have been queen for as long as Victoria. I'll bet the Prince
is wishing she'd drop dead so he could take over the job.''

"Cripes, who wants to be a king these days?" Jim said.

"Shut up, damn it," Buffalo Dong said. "Hank, what
about badgering the Queen?''

Hank laughed. "Our boy, Hector, has really brought
one up from the bottom of the grab bag. He's claiming that
the Treaty of Paris, in 1783, was illegal since King George
was nutty as a fruitcake and incapable of signing such a
treaty.''

"Treaty of Paris?" Jim said, scowling, even as he munched his small candy bar.

Marcy said, "The treaty which ended the Revolutionary War and gave the thirteen colonies their independence. And Hector's right, as far as that goes. The king was around the bend."

"At any rate," Hank laughed, "Hector's claiming that since the king was in no shape to sign such a document, it's invalid and what is now the United States is actually still part of England's colonies overseas. And, as a result, we Apaches are loyal subjects of the Queen and not subject to other law."

"Hell," Jim said. "I thought we were loyal subjects of the French, either them or the Mexicans."

"Okay, okay," Buffalo Dong said. "So what else is new? Yesterday, we were loyal greasers or frogs, now we're loyal limies."

"Don't forget we're also Russians from Siberia," Marcy put in.

Hank said, fiddling with his dials some more, "This is all getting to be more of a mess by the minute."

And Marcy said, twisting her mouth, "If you can keep your head when those about you are losing theirs—perhaps you've misunderstood the situation. Or, to put it in a different way; when in doubt, worry."

"Here's something," Hank said to Buffalo Dong. "After a big shootout with the FBI, you've been captured in Los Angeles. They burnt down the better part of a city block getting you."

"Fer crissakes," the chief said. "I hope they don't kill the guy before they find out the mistaken identity. Could it be one of our people?"

Marcy said, "I don't think we have anybody in L.A."

Hank said, "Here's a report from the Reunited Nations. The Third World delegates are sounding off for us again. All about Yankee Imperialism and Colonialism. They're calling for a boycott of all American international dealings in uranium."

"You can always depend on the Third World," Marcy said.

"And here's a related item," Hank said. "This is good. Teams of uranium prospectors have swarmed over Geronimo County, now that it's definite that we all pulled out of the reservation. They're locating all sorts of rich uranium deposits."

"Uh-oh," said Buffalo Dong. "That'll chill any chances of our coming to terms for awhile."

Jim looked over at him. "Well, damn it, wasn't that what we were expecting?"

"Yeah," the older man said gloomily. "I suppose so. But those who figured out our whole strategy aren't out in the field like we are. Do you realize that there's enough damn troops in this State now to conquer South America?"

"Yeah," Hank said in turn. "What're we going to do about it?"

Buffalo Dong took a deep breath. "We're going to have to clear out, kids. It's getting too hot. It's just a matter of time before we run into some of these trigger-happy jerks and they'll blow us halfway to Kansas before we have a chance to surrender. For all practical purposes, that slob, General Phartschmeller, has ordered his troops to fire on sight. You could be wrapped up in a white flag 'til you looked like a Bedouin, and they'd fill you so full of holes you'd resemble an open door."

"Clear out to where?" Jim said bitterly. "This whole

damn country is so full of soldiers it looks like Times Square on New Year's."

Buffalo Dong thought about it.

"We can go south," he said finally. "Our reservation's in the northern part of the state and most of the action has been up here so far. There's an isolated town there I was stationed near for awhile when I was taking my army training. I got to know the country pretty well. We might hide out there. The people are amost exclusively Mexican-Americans. They don't like the Anglos much better than we do."

"What's the name of this town?"

"Coronado. Come on, it's getting dusk. Let's get under way. We don't dare try to liberate another helio-hopper. We're going to have to walk it."

They began to shrug into their equipment and take up their assault rifles.

Marcy said piously, "Kismet is but a defrocked prophet, strolling with one foot in the Galilee of time."

"Gee," Hank said, looking at her in mock questioning. "I thought you said it was an odorous turd."

"No, that was *life*. This is *Kismet*."

Chapter Seventeen

John Shay checked out not only the dossier of Nora Chutzpa, whose original name turned out to be Nora Rose Stebbins, but also the dossiers of all the Chutzpa family. He was surprised to find out how little was available on the Chutzpas. Not even the medical records in the National Data Banks, nor the educational records of the younger family members, were of any help. This might have been understandable so far as the elders were concerned, since they had spent their early years before the advent of the National Data Banks, but not the kids.

He came to a partial answer when he discovered that one Chutzpa had an M.D. and another had a degree in education. The doctor had never received an appointment from the computers to practice, and the potential teacher had never been given a job in education. However, it was to be assumed that both were competent to handle such matters in a family no larger than the Chutzpas.

He also checked out everything he could find on the family soul-farm, as they were being called these days. And there was precious little on *that*, either; no more than was absolutely demanded by law. All the red-tape material needed for them to homestead the land had been properly handled, of course, and Shay found no irregularities in the various building permits and inspections of sanitary facilities. Otherwise, the Chutzpa family was living as near to an undocumented hermit's life as seemed possible in a modern society.

When he was all through, Shay leaned back from the screen he had been concentrating on for the past several hours and thought about his findings. When the Director had mentioned playing it by ear, he couldn't have used a more apt term. There was no other way to play it.

However, Shay had gleaned one useful fact. With the exception of one old duffer, pushing sixty now, there wasn't anybody on the soul-farm that seemed likely to give Shay any physical threat. This Joseph Chutzpa had been in the army, way back during the Asian War. Otherwise, the male residents hadn't a single thing in their dossiers to indicate they'd ever seen a weapon deadlier than a fly swatter. There were no weapons registered in the family's possession, not even a shotgun or a .22 rifle. There was no record of the two younger men, Zack and Ronald, ever having participated in any sports at all, certainly not boxing or wrestling. Neither of them had any criminal record whatsoever, not even some youthful peccadillo such as a car theft. Nor did anyone else in the family, for that matter. In short, they were as vulnerable a bunch of cubes as could be found.

Inwardly, John Shay grunted his sour version of amusement. He had no criminal record either.

He considered his approach for awhile, finally dialed the local Ultra-Market on the phone screen, and requested its liquor list. He was no authority on exotic potables and wound up ordering a dozen bottles of the most expensive stuff in the small Coronado distribution center. He put his universal credit card in the payment slot and requested immediate delivery.

When they arrived in the room's delivery box, in a small carton, he took the bottles up, one by one, and examined them. There were such items as Benedictine, Irish Mist, Chartreuse, Calvados and Drambuie. He rewrapped them neatly, in the tissue in which they had come, and carried the carton out to his rented car. He then returned to the room and carefully selected from his one large piece of luggage the most informal clothing he had on hand.

Dressed in this, he put his Universal Credit Card in the room's payment slot, paid his lodging bill, carried his bag out to the car and took off for the Chutzpa estate. It was early afternoon. He was playing it by ear—as ordered.

He had the exact location of the Chutzpa soul-farm from the National Data Banks. He didn't want to have to ask directions. He preferred that nobody in Coronado even knew that he had gone there.

To his surprise there was no road, or even a country path, leading out to the underground dwellings. The approach looked more like a golf fairway than anything else. It would seem that the Chutzpas used hover vehicles whenever possible and that if, occasionally, an old four-wheeler was utilized, each time it was driven in over a slightly different route to avoid wearing permanent ruts. Hence, there were no signs of a road. They must even have walked over different routes, each time they passed.

But Shay didn't have any difficulty locating the main

dwelling. He parked in front of it, in such manner that if a quick escape was required, he could jump into his vehicle and take off without any preliminary backing and turning. He sat there for a moment, taking in the layout. The Barn and The Kid's Kolony he located, in spite of their natural camouflage. He decided correctly that they were auxiliary buildings. There didn't seem to be any complications so far.

John Shay got out of his rental car, took up the carton of fancy liquor and headed for the steps down into the patio.

Once there, he began yelling, "Hello, hello! Where's everybody?" in as hearty a voice as he could muster.

There was only one person, stretched out on a hand-crafted chair, in the patio sun. She was scowling over some publication that looked like one of the government releases on the management of small farms.

She looked up and said, "Hello. Who in the devil are you?"

John Shay grinned down at her, the carton of booze balanced on one shoulder. "I'm Jack," he said. "Nora sent me."

"Christ," she said, coming to her feet and tossing the pamphlet down onto the chair she'd just deserted. "Come on in. I'm Rusty."

His smile wavered for a moment. "You're what?"

"Not what. Who. My name's Rusty."

"Oh. Oh, yeah. You must be Rebecca. Nora told me about you. I'm anxious to meet you all. You're practically the only thing Nora ever talks about."

The slightest of frowns momentarily crossed Rusty's freckled face but she said, "Come on in and meet whoever's around. At this time of the day, they might be anywhere. How's Nora? It's been a long time."

"Oh, she's swell. That's one girl I hate to leave."

Rusty shot another look at him but led the way to the saloon.

The only ones there were the Doc, the Professor, Moon, Ron and JoJo—if dogs weren't to be counted. All looked up at the advent of the newcomer.

Rusty said heartily, "Here's a friend of Nora's. By the looks of him, bearing gifts, like a Greek. Though he doesn't look like a Greek. He looks perfectly normal."

Moon favored Rusty with a subtle glance as he came to his feet to greet the newcomer. Of them all, he alone had caught the impact of her quote from Virgil: *I fear the Greeks, even when bearing gifts.*

John Shay put the carton down on the table and shook hands all around. He said, grinning, "Now, don't tell me. You're Donald, the doctor. And you're Alfred. And, of course; you're either Ronald or Zack."

"I'm Ron," that one said, smiling.

They all shook, cheerfully enough, but the Doc said, "They call me Doc." He looked at the Professor. "Is your name Alfred, for Christ's sake?"

"Yes, of course. But, good grief, it's been a long time since I was called that."

Moon came up, following Ron, and the newcomer frowned. "I don't believe I remember Nora mentioning you."

Moon shook his head. "I'm a newcomer." After exchanging standard greetings he looked down into the carton. "Holy smokes," he said. "Sippin' liquor. We won't have to drink Doc's rotgut for awhile."

"You bastard," Doc said indignantly. "You're the biggest lush on the place. You've put such a hole in my, ah, cellars, I'll have to get back to fermenting and distilling."

Moon put his hand over his heart as though in pure innocence. "Lush?" he said in reproach. "I'll have you know I never drink anything thick enough to chew."

The stranger flicked his eyes back and forth between them but gave up and turned to JoJo, who was standing slightly to one side, her eyes wide and her lips slightly parted. "Oh, good heavens," she said in excitement, "You mean that you've just come from my mother?"

Shay came over to her, smiling widely. "You must be JoJo. You're as pretty as Nora ever said you were." He took her by the shoulders and awkwardly kissed her on one cheek, which she gladly presented.

Rusty looked over at the Professor and raised her eyebrows slightly. The glance caught his own. He too looked somewhat puzzled. Neither of them knew that Moon had, in turn, caught their exchange.

John Shay went over to the carton on the table and brought forth one of the squat tissue-wrapped bottles. On the way, he almost tripped over Bowser. He looked down in irritation. "Hey, get out of the way. I don't like mutts."

Bowser got, then sat down to one side and looked at the newcomer, the tip of his red tongue out. "Then we're even-steven," he said nastily.

Shay stared down at the dog, his composure momentarily rocking on its heels.

The Doc said, "A gag. Ummm, just a gag. What did you say your name was?"

"Jack," Shay told him. "Jack Shay. How about a quick one, everybody?" He shot another sideways look at the moth-eaten pup.

"I'll get glasses," Ron said, heading for the bar.

While they were waiting, Rusty said, "How long are you here for . . . Jack?"

Shay said, sinking into a chair, "Mind if I sit down? Kind of tired. Oh, I don't know. When I told Nora I'd be driving through this part of the country, she insisted I stop off long enough to get to know you folks. She and I have a thing going, and, well, she insisted that I get to know you."

"Great," the Professor said. "Good grief, Benedictine. This is a helluva time of day for Benedictine but let's open it. I haven't tasted the stuff for twenty years."

Ron had returned with the glasses and for a moment they were occupied with pouring.

JoJo said, "This is wonderful. I've just applied for my GAS and couldn't prove anything about my parents. But now I'll know all about mother. Her real name—everything."

"Oh, sure," Shay said with a sweep of his hand. "Her name was Nora Rose Stebbins and she was born in South Neward, Maine, in 1970. She's about forty now. But she sure doesn't look it."

Moon held up his glass in a toast. "First one today . . ." He paused and added, "with this hand."

They all laughed and took a sip of their drinks.

Blackie came in from the kitchen and said, wiping her hands on an apron, "What the hell's going on?"

The Professor told her, "Friend of Nora's came through. We ought to talk him into staying at least a few days. Especially since he's brought all this fancy sippin' likker." He peered into the carton. "Good grief, there must be a month's GAS credits in there." He looked up at Shay.

The newcomer shrugged it off. "I'm not on GAS. I had the good luck to inherit a chunk of pseudo-dollars and from time to time I get in on a good thing." Outwardly Shay was all charm and good will.

Zack had come in from the patio just in time to hear Shay. Even before introductions he said, "Good thing? How do you mean?"

Shay stood and grinned—he was getting tired of grinning, and felt like an idiot—and said, "You must be Zack. Nora mentioned you. I mean investments that come along if you've got a little in the way of pseudo-dollar credits. We've still, uh, got some free enterprise even if they do call it People's Capitalism these days."

Moon looked over at him thoughtfully at that, but the newcomer didn't catch it, nor Rusty's appraisal.

Zack said, "Golly, that's for me. I've got one or two ideas in the working. Maybe you can give me some background on how to develop them."

"Sure," Shay said. "Have a drink."

Blackie said, "Hell, this is wonderful. We haven't seen Nora in years. JoJo was just a little girl. Now, let me see. We can put you up in the Kid's Kolony."

Zack said quickly, "He could bunk in with me. I've got double beds in my room."

Shay said, "It's not important but I'd just as well sleep alone." He pretended embarrassment. "I snore."

Zack began something, but Blackie said, "All right. You can take over Sweet Alice's room in the Kolony and Sweet Alice can move in with Zack . . . or somebody."

Moon was looking down into the carton of booze. He said, "Holy smokes, Metaxa. Who ever heard of Metaxa in this day and age?" He brought the bottle forth.

Shay said, magnanimously, "Crack it, crack it."

And Bowser said nastily, "You didn't bring a bone, did you?"

The newcomer stared down at him again, disconcerted, and then up at the Doc accusingly. But nobody bothered to set him straight. It was Moon's joke; let him handle it any way he liked.

They had more drinks and then the Doc and Blackie brought forth a profusion of sandwiches and they had more drinks with them, some resorting to the chilled hard cider by this time. Additional members of the family drifted in until all were present and all had met the newcomer. And they talked about Nora and the old days, and the newcomer, Jack, seemed to know more about her and what she'd been doing of recent years than any of them. It made for a bang-up evening. It was seldom that the family had a complete stranger on the scene.

JoJo in particular was happy about it all. She said, "I'll have to phone Max Cohn to come tomorrow and find out what he needs to know about my family." She frowned, charmingly. "He left in an awful hurry this morning. As though something was the matter. I can't imagine what."

Later, in the middle of the animated conversation, Moon and Bowser went out for a breath of air and what Moon called a Pee Patrol for the dog. Rusty, yawning—supposedly from all the drinks—went along.

They mounted the steps into the fresh mountain air and walked silently for a moment.

"It doesn't hang together, Moon," she said finally.

"What?"

"Nora's a Lesbian. She even tried to brace me, just before she left."

"I thought she was JoJo's mother."

"Yeah. She was still young when she was here with us. All confused. She'd evidently made a try at being at least bi-sexual, and became pregnant. And JoJo was the result. But Nora didn't like the child. In fact, she hated her. It was one of the reasons she never liked it here. None of us really liked her, and she didn't like us. She wasn't our people, Moon."

"I see. So our boy isn't exactly telling a straight story about him and Nora?"

"It doesn't ring true in a dozen different directions. For instance, I've been here forever, but I never knew that the Professor's name was Alfred, and I've just about forgotten that the Doc's real name was Donald. I'm sure that Nora never knew their real names. If she had, in this length of time she would've forgotten them. He also knew my name's Rebecca, and nobody's called me that since before Nora ever came here."

"I got a feeling of something off-beat. But I couldn't exactly put my finger on it. I'm almost as much of a stranger as he is."

Rusty said, after they'd walked some more, "That fellow's come for you, hasn't he?"

Moon looked at her, evaluating, then said, "Yeah. I suppose he has."

"To arrest you?"

He thought about that. "No. I guess not. Otherwise, he'd have already done it."

"To kill you?"

Moon shrugged. "It's possible."

"What's your real name?"

"Instead of Moon? Lawrence. Lawrence Mullins."

"No. I mean your real name. Christ, people don't come to kill men named Moon Mullins. He's a professional, isn't he?"

"Oh." He thought about it some more. "Yeah, he's probably a pro. My real name is Ross Prager."

"You're in trouble, I take it?"

"The worst kind," he chuckled. "I'm a writer."

"A writer? Do they kill writers these days?"

"A political writer." He made a face and rubbed a dark hand back over his short hair. "Yes. They kill political writers in all ages."

"The family's pretty much for you . . . Ross."

"Yeah. I'll try and clear out."

She looked up at him.

He sighed and said, "Like I said, he's probably a pro, Rusty. And probably has government backing. I didn't come here to cause you trouble."

"Aren't *you* armed?"

"No. I do my fighting with a voco-typer, not a gun."

"What's holding you up? Why don't you just lam out right now?"

"I've got to check with Franny. I don't know where she is tonight. Probably checking things out in Coronado."

"What in the devil's she got to do with it?"

"She's riding shotgun for me."

Rusty stared at him. "What's that supposed to mean?"

Moon sucked in air. "I'm not very sharp as a fugitive. I'm kind of on the vague and disorganized side. Franny's taking care of me. The theory is, I can't be bothered with details. I've got to be free to think."

Rusty held her head back and glared up at the stars in appeal to higher powers. "Christ! A big sonofabitch like *you*?" She saw that she had embarrassed him and quickly shifted focus. "And *Franny*?" she said. "She's the biggest scatterbrain this side of . . ."

"You don't know Franny as well as you think you do," he told her. "She probably puts on a different front when she's out here with you people."

"Why does she come?" she said slowly.

He looked over at her. "I suspect that she thinks people

like you are the future—or, at least, an important part of it." He hesitated. "Besides, she loves you all."

She had no immediate answer to that.

He added, "I doubt if she'd leave the Wizard, her own son, here unless she figured it was a better atmosphere than he'd find among her rocket-set people, her relatives and so forth."

"All right, all right," she sighed. "But let's get back to this guy Jack. Why don't you just light out? Right this minute, without even getting your luggage. Hide someplace; Franny can join you later."

"Because it's up to her to make those decisions. She's in contact with the National Executive Committee. She might know something I don't. Possibly this guy Jack isn't alone. Maybe he's got some friends down the road waiting for Franny and me to make a break for it. Lots of possibilities—all of 'em unpleasant."

She stopped abruptly and faced him. "You're some kind of a bigwig, aren't you? I mean, a really big one."

He was embarrassed again. "I wish I thought so. But some people think I am."

Chapter Eighteen

John Shay awoke early and from no deep dream of peace. His session with the Chutzpa family had lasted late into the night and no matter how hard he'd tried, he couldn't keep completely from imbibing. It would have been too conspicuous, especially since he had attempted to put over a picture of himself as a real swinger, who hung out with Nora in one of the most far-out communes in the Catskill Mountains.

What had awakened him now was a squirming in the bed. He sat up abruptly, on full alert, and his hand darted beneath the pillow for the gun he'd had altered to his own specifications. But then he blinked and snarled, "What-in-the-*hell* are you doing here?"

It was the nine-year-old, Ruthie. She and the Twins had been sent off to bed early, and the bespectacled, objectionable little Wizard not long afterward. A few hours later, Sweet Alice had taken him over to her room in what they called the Kid Kolony. She evidently stayed there, more or less baby-sitting the youngest members of the family, though she herself must have been only in her middle teens. She'd made it rather clear that she was willing to stay on for the night. However, nothing was further from his mind. He didn't mess with women while on a contract. Besides, he wanted no complications with the Chutzpa family. He had no idea who might get sore if he ripped off a piece with this blonde blank-brain. He wanted everything to be as pleasantly innocent as could be, until he had finished his assignment—preferably ''accidentally''—and was on his way. So he'd declined as gently as possible, not wishing to antagonize her either, and claimed exhaustion. Sweet Alice didn't seem upset by the rejection; merely yawned and muttered something about seeing what Ron was doing, and was gone.

But now, *this* kid! Blue jazus, if one of the adult Chutzpas came in and found her in his bed, there'd be hell to pay.

She said, trying to make her voice sultry, ''I thought you might be lonesome, or cold . . . or something.''

''Well, I'm not! Now scoot on out of here, or I'll spank you.''

Her eyes narrowed sensuously. ''You want to spank me?'' She rolled over onto her stomach. ''Not too hard, mind.''

He rolled his eyes upward. ''Get the hell out of here!'' he ordered, giving her a none too gentle shove and keeping up the pressure until she had scrambled out to the floor.

She was dressed in the most inadequate shorty night-gown he could ever remember having seen, even on an adult, even on a whore. She made a coquettish shrug of her childish body and swayed from the room. "You'll be sorry you . . . rejected me," she said, even a bit nastily.

When she was gone he shook his head, then sat up and put it in his hands. What an outfit. Some of the details of the previous night came back to him.

He'd gotten into a conversation with Ron, evidently the young intellectual of the family. The kid had been studying up on hemp and its various derivatives and when he'd asked Shay if he knew anything about them, the hit man had decided he couldn't plead complete ignorance, in view of his supposed high life with Nora.

Evidently, the family had a plot of *Cannabis Sativa,* as Ron called it, and used it on occasion for making both cigarettes and hashish fudge. But Ron had found a passage that intrigued him in one of his books. It seemed that in Nepal, where the best hemp was grown, they had a particular way of extracting the resin which developed on the flowering tops even before the tiny greenish flowers were ready to bloom. They'd send completely naked people running pell-mell through the hot, steaming rows of hemp and what resin stuck to them was later scraped off to become the ultra-powerful *Charas,* the purest form of hashish.

What stymied Ron was choosing someone to run bare-assed naked through the hemp plants.

He had said thoughtfully, "Maybe we could get Sweet Alice to do it. She'll do anything."

Shay had extracted himself from the conversation as best he could, only to get into an even more complicated one with Zack, who wanted details on how to get onto a good thing, how to know how to see one when it presented itself and how to exploit it. In actuality, Shay knew even less on this subject than he had about exotic means of extracting hashish.

Yes, Shay had spent one hell of a confusing evening.

He got up now and looked about the room that had been turned over to him. It was comfortable enough and only vaguely on the feminine side, though it was originally the abode of the far-out blonde. He went into the hall and located the bath, which was constructed on a child's level. He made do, only partially thrown off when one of the twins, bleary with sleep, toddled in and answered the call of nature, right beside him.

Back in Sweet Alice's room again, Shay looked out the window and noted that it was still not long after dawn. It was an opportunity to get an idea of the whole place. He doubted if anyone else would be up and around, in view of the strenuous night before. He slipped into slacks, a short shirt and tennis shoes, tucked his .38 Recoilless into his belt, beneath the shirt, and let himself out. The layout of the Kid Kolony was similar to that of the larger dwelling in which the adult members slept. He had no difficulty in finding his way to the surface.

But if Shay thought he was going to be able to stroll around the layout without hindrance, he was mistaken. He was hailed almost immediately by the lardy specimen they called Doc.

"Hi," Doc called, coming up. "Another early bird, eh? Ummm, you know, I always get up at dawn, no matter when I went to bed. Best time of the day."

"Yeah," Shay said. It was the first daybreak he had seen in ten years, and last time it had been only because he had been staked out with a sawed-off shotgun, awaiting a victim who had been reported as an early morning jogger.

Doc said, "Come along. I'll show you my winery,

brewery, and distillery—the booze-works. Most important project on the place.''

John Shay could believe it. He fell in step. There was nothing else to do. Besides, he didn't mind the chance to get off to one side with an older member of the family. He might get some tips he could use later when he needed to live in the margins of society.

Doc led the way to The Barn, sounding off as they went.

''Ummm. You know, that fancy booze you brought yesterday is all well and good, and don't think that I don't appreciate it. But, you know, it's not the stuff you want to drink every day. It's special and, for that matter, some of it's crap.''

''Oh?'' Shay said. He'd laid out a lot of pseudo-dollars for that attempt to make points with the Chutzpa family. ''By the way, how long's this fellow Moon been here?'' To cover his question, he added, ''Nora didn't mention him.''

But Doc rambled on, ignoring the question, as they descended the steps into The Barn. ''You take that Calvados you brought, imported from France. What it really is, is applejack; apple brandy. And the stuff we make right here is *so* much better—''

''That right?'' Shay said. ''I was kind of surprised to see a nigg . . . a Black here with all you whites.''

Ignoring Shay's last remark, Doc led the way to a large room which smelled of sour apples, of rotten apples, of fermenting apples, of . . . apples. ''Applejack is a science. I was weaned on applejack.''

Shay gave up for the moment probing about Moon. ''What's applejack?'' he made the mistake of saying.

Doc beamed, his fat face happy at the opportunity to

answer. "It's just one more example proving that people no longer give a shit what they eat or drink. It's like everything came out of a god-damned delivery tube out of a factory. You take potato chips."

"Potato chips?" the other said blankly. What, in the name of blue jazus, had their conversation to do with potato chips?

"Potato chips. They take ten cents worth of potatoes and fry them in a couple of cents worth of dubious oil and then sprinkle *much* too much salt on them and package them up in plastic with a lot of crap advertising on the bag and sell them for almost two pseudo-dollars a pound. If you have a brain in your head, you'll buy the potatoes fresh, go to the horrible labor—everybody these days seems to think—of peeling them yourself, fry them in some decent oil, soybean, peanut, sesame, anything'll do, and wind up with better potato chips for one tenth, or less, the cost. But no, that's not the way the American mind . . ."

"Well, about this applejack," Shay said. They had come up to a moderately large cider press.

"Ummm," the Doc said happily. "Now, I'll tell you how to make real applejack, real apple brandy. What you do first is raise your own damned apples. Apples ideal for cider; there's various kinds. Then you harvest them and stash them away. Apples store real well. Of course, you throw out the ones showing any rot at all. We cut them up, throwing away the bad parts and using the rest for apple butter, apple jelly, that sort of thing. So you store the apples until winter and then you squeeze them for cider. Then you let the cider go hard. That's another thing before you get to the brandy. You can take good hard cider and, if you treat it the same way they make champagne, nine people out of ten who think they like champagne can't tell the difference. But you've got to know how to do it.''

''I'll bet,'' Shay said.

''Well, you do, you know,'' the Doc said, suspicious of sarcasm. ''You've got to use the same type bottles and corks and you've got to take the time, and work out the sediment, and re-bottle it. Let me tell you, it's a chore. But you wind up with a sparkling hard cider that's as good as anything that ever swept over your tonsils.''

John Shay tried to keep from staring at the roly-poly man. The other was obviously completely sincere. He really cared about this bullshit. Well, it was his lasso, let him twirl it.

''Anyway,'' the Doc said, ''you wait until winter. Sometimes it gets twenty below around here. Then you take your hard cider and put it in a wooden barrel. Say fifty gallons or so. Then you stick it outside at night, when the freeze comes, you know. Then when you get up in the morning, it's frozen solid, at least the way it looks on top. The thing is, hard cider is possibly ten or twelve percent alcohol, no more. But when this big drop in temperature comes, the alcohol doesn't freeze. It's driven into the center of the barrel and all the rest of the crap is frozen solid. But there's the brandy in the very center. What you do is take an ice pick and chip out the top and in the middle of the barrel you've got about ten gallons or so of the most pure, most beautiful apple brandy you ever tasted. You just dip it out and bottle it. You don't even have to especially age it. It's not like it was distilled. There's no fusel oil or anything. It's ready to drink. Distilled brandy isn't anything like it.''

John Shay stared, letting his frank amazement show. ''Why'd you go to the trouble?'' he blurted.

"How do you mean?"

"You can just order a bottle of Calvados, or any other apple brandy in this country, from the ultra-market. This stuff of yours must take half the year to turn out."

"Ummm, the whole year, before you're through," the Doc said patiently. "But that's the point. It's the same with the potato chips."

He stopped for a moment, searching for a better illustration of his point. Finally he said, "It's like the notion that the way you get the best piece of ass in the world is to go to Greater Washington or Paris, and go to the swankiest hotel in town and tell the bellhop to get you one of these five hundred pseudo-dollar call girls. And she comes up in a mink coat, smelling of perfume that costs a bucket of money an ounce. And she puts out for you and you never saw her before in your life and you never see her again. Bullshit. That's not the best piece of ass in the world. Where do you think the term 'roll in the hay' came from? And, make no mistake, the best sex in the world is a roll in the hay with a girl you know, and like, and she likes you. And you're trying to see that she gets a good time out of it, and she's trying to be sure *you* do. Friend, that's *sex* and the hell with the mink coat and the perfume that whore in Paris wears."

John Shay didn't know how he'd been led off onto this tangent. He was trying to case the Chutzpa family soul-farm and to learn a little about the Black he had the contract on.

He said wearily, "That's right, and it's great for you people out here. It's your ball and you bounce it the way you want. I mean making your own applejack and all. And I guess you grow a lot of your own food—like beans and pineapples and all the things you must grow. But it doesn't apply to most people anymore,'' he said desperately. "Like shoes. You can't make your own *shoes*.''

"Like hell you can't,'' the Doc snorted, looking down at the sandals he was wearing, "What do you call these?'' Zack and Rusty are particularly good at it. You know— when the spirit moves them. But Coleen was even better, before she took that damn job in town at the ultra-market. That's what I'm talking about. People are crazy with all this automation. Sure, some of it's great, necessary, saves a lot of miserable labor, like digging in mines, that sort of thing. But something's gone out of the human race, with modern industry. In the old days, a shoemaker used to work maybe the better part of a week turning out a pair of shoes. But when they were finished, he had a product of his own labor. He could see it, feel it, be proud of it, if it was a good job, and a little sorry if he'd flubbed this pair. But today, you've got your automated shoe factories. Some technician in a white smock checks some dials and pushes a few buttons and the shoes come out of the plant by the tens of thousands. He never sees the end product. They're all wrapped and packaged and shipped—all automatically. How can he take any pride in the product of his labor? He's a goddamned clog in a machine. And next year they'll probably automate *him* out of his job, and he'll go onto GAS.''

Zack came up, obviously pleased to see the newcomer to the Chutzpa soul-farm. "Hi,'' he said. "Good morning. What spins?''

Doc growled, "What on earth are you doing up so early?''

"I was practicing with my bullwhip novelty. I think I've got some of the kinks worked out.'' The younger man had been carrying what looked like a short policeman's baton made of leather. He self-consciously stuck it in a hip pocket.

Shay was about to ask him what in the hell a bullwhip was, but Zack hurried on. "Doc, you're busy with the booze, eh? I'll take over and show Jack Sun Valley and the orchards and the fish pond and all. Besides, I thought maybe he'd be interested in investing in one or two of my novelty ideas."

"Oh, swell," Doc muttered. "Watch out for the Apaches. I heard the early newscast. They're supposed to be heading south."

Zack brushed it off. "Yeah. Also, north, west and east. There must be a million of them, to allow for all the places they've been reported. The government's put on thousands of extra guards at every nuclear power plant in the country. They're afraid Buffalo Dong's braves will try to blow 'em."

The rest of the day for 'Jack' Shay was more of the same. He was shown every nook and cranny and mud hole of the Chutzpa family's soul-farm. When one family member gave out, or had something to do, another one took over. He'd pretty well had it, by day's end, but in actuality he'd gotten what he wanted. A complete feel of the place, and a fairly good idea of most of the family members. None of them was anything to worry about. He felt secure in the belief that he could have taken the whole outfit on, had that been the Director's desire.

Fulfilling the contract "accidentally" was another thing, although he'd had ideas when the good-looking young brunette, JoJo, had taken him for a brief walk. They'd strolled away from the soul-farm, for a view of what she called the Grand Canyon of the Rio Grande. It was quite a view at that though, at this point, not nearly so spectacular

Mack Reynolds

as that of the Grand Canyon of the Colorado to the northwest. Shay had passed that once, on his business travels, but hadn't stopped for the various views. Such things bothered him. He'd been on his way to a rendez-vous with a recalcitrant gambler who the big shots back east considered redundant.

But this gave him an idea. If he could just walk the big jig out here, it shouldn't be too difficult to see that the other accidentally fell over a cliff. Particularly if he was given a little urging to fall.

He'd had the standard Chutzpa lunch and was again astonished at the abundance of food, served buffet style. Then, in the afternoon, he was taken over the soul-farm again to see goats, poultry, fish, fruit, vegetables and sundry other wonders which interested him not at all.

Yes, by evening he'd had it. Then, waiting for the evening meal which Doc was whomping up in honor of his visit, he met Max Cohn who was visiting from Coronado to get details about Nora Chutzpa for the Guaranteed Annual Stipend application.

John Shay had roughly the same regard for Jews that he did for Blacks but suppressed that and offered a flood of knowledge about Nora Stebbins which he had acquired through his special access to the National Data Banks.

Cohn, he decided, was one of *those*. When Max looked at JoJo, he looked like a sick calf, though John Shay had never seen a calf, indisposed or otherwise. Max Cohn was another meaningless cipher. No danger in him.

Now, the woman introduced to him as Franny might be another thing, though he doubted it, being aware of her background as the notorious rocket-set gadabout. She was older than he had expected, from the occasional shots he had seen of her in the newscasts, but for him she didn't project much. In dress and manner she differed only a little from the other women members of the family.

Nevertheless, he had an uneasy feeling about her. Almost as though she was onto him—but how could she be? His cover was damned near perfect. She had known Nora; had been in contact with her, by phone at least, fairly recently. But she didn't have the information about the woman at her fingertips that he did. Hell, he knew how many of Nora's teeth were still in her head. So screw Franny.

The evening progressed much as had the previous one. These people had a knack for talking up a storm about the widest variety of crap that John Shay had ever run into. The whole bunch seemed more interested in talking than they did in watching Tri-Di, which any normal gathering would have been doing. In fact, he'd never seen the big Tri-Di set turned on since he had arrived.

The kid, Ron, cornered him for awhile and explained the latest writing project he was on. Ron had arrived at a theory pertaining to dirty jokes, and particularly limericks. According to Ron Chutzpa, the old question about who originated such material was easily answerable. He gave a rundown on the seeming genius that went into composing dirty limericks, adding his contention that Shakespeare himself would have been barely equal to the task. Ron's answer was that nobody, no individuals, composed them; they were a development of many minds.

John Shay couldn't have cared less. He was no connoisseur of jokes, dirty or otherwise, limericks or any other form. Shay's uninterest, of course, didn't put off the aspiring writer for a moment.

Ron gave an example. According to his research, one

famed limerick had gone back to the days when even
Bitter Joe, the family elder, was a youngster. It had gone:

> *There was a young man from Racine,*
> *Who invented a screwing machine.*
> *Both concave and convex,*
> *It would screw either sex.*
> *It was the damndest machine ever seen.*

But then, contended Ron, the limerick had been developed by persons unknown, in various directions, adding to its effectiveness. The last line had become, variously:

> *But it was a helluva thing to clean.*
> *And would jerk itself off, in between.*

Or, the British version.

> *And guaranteed used by the Queen.*

Shay said, trying to go along, "Well, so what? What'd
you figure on doing with this, uh, earthshaking research?"

Ron was triumphant. "I figure on developing each limerick to an additional point, a more complete and satisfac-
tory point."

Shay looked at him blankly. "Like how?"

"Well, take the last version. The British one. I'm im-
proving on it."

"I'm listening."

Ron cleared his throat and recited:

> *A patriotic young Scott from Skean,*
> *Dedicated his screwing machine.*
> *(Both concave and convex,*
> *It would screw either sex)*
> *By Appointment to Her Majesty, the Queen.*

Shay ogled him. Without thinking, he had taken a slug
of the sparkling hard cider, though he was hardly over the
hangover of that morning. Doc had insisted he try it. He

said, "Well, what are you going to do with all this, uh, stuff?"

"I'm going to write a book," Ron said. "Take this other old-timer I've updated. You've probably heard the first version already:

> *There was a young fellow named Durkin,*
> *Who was always jerkin' his gherkin.*
> *Said his father to Durkin, "Stop*
> *Jerkin' your gherkin.*
> *Your gherkin's fer ferkin', not jerkin'.*

"Oh," said Shay.

"Now, the way I've improved it is this," Ron said happily.

> *There once was a man named Durkin,*
> *Who was always jerkin' his gherkin.*
> *Said his wife, one day,*
> *Deprived of her lay,*
> *"Durkin, you're shirkin' your ferkin' by jerkin' your*
> *Gherkin, you bastard.*

Shay said weakly, "That last line. It doesn't even rhyme."

"Yeah, that's the point. Now, here's another one. About the Pope."

Shay finally escaped the would-be poet and for a time, avoided personal conversation by sitting in on a diatribe by Bitter Joe against circumcision. Poor Max Cohn sat there uncomfortably, obviously fearful of saying something that might upset a member of his beloved's family.

"It's all a lot of damn superstition," the bitter one was proclaiming. "Started in Central Africa and worked itself down the Nile with the Egyptians. The Hebrews picked it up there and have been proclaiming it God's will ever since. Crap. If nature didn't want man to have a foreskin she wouldn't have hung one on the end of his pecker.

Female circumcision is even sillier. Still prevails, in Africa. They cut the poor girl's clitoris off, for Christ sake.''

Moon, who was also listening in, said, "At least, circumcision makes an unbeatable argument against Lysenko."

"Who?" Bitter Joe scowled.

"The Russian geneticist. He opposed the theories of heredity; supported the doctrine that characteristics acquired through environmental influences are inherited. For some reason, Joe Stalin seemed to think that was Marxist, so it became the Soviet science party line."

Max said, "But . . . but what's that got to do with circumcision?"

Moon looked over at him. "Did you ever see a Jewish boy born circumcised?"

It was then that the evening session of the Chutzpa family in the saloon was interrupted.

A short, wiry figure stood in the doorway to the patio. The black braided hair was down to the shoulders and there was a dirty leather thong around the forehead. Across the nose and extended to both cheeks was a smear of white war paint. In the intruder's hands was a heavy, awkward-looking rifle. Behind him, two others loomed, similarly armed and painted.

"Ugh," the newcomer grunted. "White man and squaws and papooses my prisoners."

Chapter Nineteen

All eyes were on the three. Behind them came a girl, also obviously an Indian, though somewhat neater than the men and sans war paint.

The leader said, "Ugh. Me Buffalo Dong, War Chief of the Marijuanero Apaches. My braves have whole place surrounded."

Blackie had been seated in a rocker, knitting. "Bullshit," she said placidly.

The four Indians stared at her.

"Ugh. What?" Buffalo Dong said.

"I said bullshit. The place isn't surrounded. There's only the four of you."

The leader of the painted Indians looked more dangerous. "Ugh. White squaw talk with forked tongue. My braves all over place. You try to escape, braves killum."

All eyes went back to Blackie, who continued to knit.

She said comfortably, "I'll tell you something about

this soul-farm, Mr. Buffalo Dong. It's surrounded by trees, mostly fruit and nut trees, but shade and lumber too. One of the first things we planted. Good windbreak, for one thing, also a refuge for bird and animal life. The thing is, we raise guinea fowl. A lot of them. At night, they roost in the trees. They're the best alarms in the world. They could hear a mouse coming up, not to speak of a whole damned bunch of Indians. They make a helluva racket. Sounds like they're squawking *Pay your taxes. Pay your taxes.* If somebody comes to the front door the regular way, like you four did, it doesn't bother them. But if there was a pack of you bozos crawling around this place, our guinea fowl would be sounding off this minute, loud enough to raise the dead.''

The four Indians continued to stare at her, disconcerted.

Blackie went on evenly, ''Besides, there couldn't be many more of you anyway, what with all of your supposed political refugees in Mexico, France, Switzerland, and representatives to the Reunited Nations, doing public relations in England, and the delegations to all the major world countries asking for diplomatic recognition. And all of them young or middle-aged people. The Wizard has been keeping me informed on the whole thing. He loves to talk and nobody else will listen but Sweet Alice and she doesn't understand what he says. Where are you keeping your old folks and the kids? I'll bet my ass that they're in places like New York, Chicago and, say, New Orleans. Big cities with a high percentage of ethnic groups with dark skins. Probably visiting friends and relatives. The ideal places to hide until everything's blown over.''

Marcy demanded, ''How'd you guess?''

Bowser said nastily, ''The only good Indian is a dead Indian.''

Buffalo Dong glared around. "Ugh," he growled. "Who said that?"

"General Sherman," said Bowser. He stuck his red tongue out and gave a triple pant.

Buffalo Dong recovered first from this canine flank attack. He looked up from the dog and around, his painted face accusing. "Who's the damned ventriloquist around here?" he said dangerously.

Bowser said, "You forgot to say 'Ugh'."

Marcy was the first to laugh. "Shoot the dog," she cracked, "he knows too much."

"Bowser's a Sazarac," Zack said, as though that explained all.

Bitter Joe had been staring at the leader of the four Indian intruders. "Hey," he blurted. "Aren't you old Sarge Eskiminzin, used to be with B Platoon?"

Buffalo Dong stared back. "I'll be damned," he said. "Wait a minute. Don't tell me. It's old Fuck-off Joe. I thought you'd copped one, there in the Delta."

"Naw," Bitter Joe said, coming to his feet to shake hands. "Just a scratch. They sent me to Bangkok for R&R. I got a dose of VD there that was worse than the hit."

Hank and Jim grounded their assault rifles and sighed in resignation.

"Cripes. Some war party," Jim muttered.

Sweet Alice came over to the younger Indians and said sympathetically, "You boys look awful with all that grease paint on your faces. Want me to show you the bathroom, and you can wash up?"

Marcy slumped down into a chair and said in sorrow, "Now I've seen it all. Everything. I tell you, everything."

Doc, climbing to his feet, said, "You know, you ought

to get out of those wigs. In this weather, you must be sweltering. As a doctor, I can tell you, you'll get heat rash.'' He headed for the bar. "How about a drink? You look like you could use one.''

Colleen said indignantly, "More likely something to eat. Why, you all look famished.''

Marcy grinned ruefully. "You ain't just a-whistlin' Dixie, white girl,'' she said.

Rusty, always practical, said, "Come on, Colleen, we'll rustle up some sandwich things to tide them over until Doc has supper finished.'' She headed for the kitchen.

Franny, who had been seated near John Shay, looked over at him. He was slightly forward in his chair, narrow-eyed, alert. Unconsciously, his right hand was clawed and only inches from the edge of his jacket.

Franny said to him evenly, "It doesn't look as though you'll need that.''

His eyes went quickly to her. "What?'' he said, relaxing the hand and dropping it to his lap. "What're you talking about?''

She didn't answer him but got up and went over to the Indian girl, who was already surrounded by Sweet Alice and JoJo. Franny said, "Come on, we'll get you a preliminary shower and some fresh clothes. You look as though you've slept in those.''

Marcy laughed bitterly. "For a week,'' she said. "The last time I had a change was when we raided a clothing shop in a deserted ski resort. But I'll have that preliminary drink first, if the offer's still good.''

Bitter Joe was saying, "I'll be damned, Sarge, you mean to tell me you're this Buffalo Dong we've been hearing about? Never occurred to me. Then you must've been the one who got all the medals after I left the company."

"Yeah," Buffalo Dong said. "I think they gave them to me because I was an Indian. Good publicity. All I ever really did was try and keep from getting my ass shot off." He knocked back the king-size slug of applejack which Doc had urged on him. "Wow," he said. "Now, that's what I call firewater, with a capital F."

The evening deteriorated into a typical Chutzpa family verbal jam session. To the blank amazement of John Shay, Max Cohn and even Moon, the whole family seemed to have accepted the situation with hardly a second thought. Welcoming this break from routine.

The Indians were overwhelmed with quick drinks and then marched off to the community bathroom for good hot baths. They were then garbed in standard family wear, denim or homespun shorts and shirts, or halters, as the case might be. Marcy turned out to have a dream of a figure, when outfitted by Sweet Alice, and both Ron and Zack hovered over her as though the only important question in their lives was how quickly they could get her into the nearest bed. Only Max was taken aback by that. Shay didn't give a damn. Moon was inwardly amused. He was rapidly becoming used to the family's sexual mores—or the absence of them.

Food followed drinks, or at least accompanied them. And where the sandwiches left off and the dinner began was a bit difficult to decide. But the flow of drinks didn't diminish.

Jim, momentarily off to one side with Hank, both with glasses in hand, said under his breath, "Hey, you don't think there's any chance of them trying to get us smashed so they can do us in, do you?"

Hank shot him a contemptuous look. "If so, it's okay with me. I'm so tired of being on the run, I could put up with having the bottom of my feet burned by old Roy Thomas' boys, if I could have a couple more hours of this treatment under my belt. Do you realize, we'll probably wind up in bed tonight? I mean a real bed, with pillows, and all those things you remember from childhood? It seems to me that all I remember since childhood is pounding around after Buffalo Dong."

"That's not what I'm remembering," Jim said. "That dizzy blonde, a few minutes ago, when nobody was looking, kind of grabbed me by the . . ."

"Watch it, watch it," Hank said. "Easy on the volume. This booze we're not used to. But that dizzy blonde, as you call her—and I warn you, you're talking about the woman I love—grabbed me about half an hour ago. By the looks of her, there's plenty for both of us, though."

"There doesn't have to be," the other member of the Indian war party said. "These are really far-out people. Now you take that Colleen. She's just as friendly . . ."

"You take her," Hank said. "Holy mother of the Great Spirit, have you seen that ever-loving brunette?"

"Yeah. But evidently there's something going between her and the stupid one. The one wearing a tie. You know, I haven't seen anyone wearing a tie, except in family portraits, for . . ."

"He's not stupid. He's just in love. I don't blame him. Talk about nourishing pussy . . ."

"Watch your mouth, you goddamned ignorant redskin, here comes that old biddy, Blackie. Hell, if she was twenty years younger I'll bet . . ."

"Twenty years younger?" Hank said indignantly. "Ten hours ago, you would have been panting after her. And she'd still probably give you a working over like you haven't had for months.''

''It feels like years,'' the other said, under his breath, as the elder of the Chutzpas came up with a tray of tasties. ''A nice fat sheep would have looked good yesterday.''

Blackie said, in matronly fashion, ''I'll bet I know what you boys are talking about.'' She smiled her placid smile. ''You were all worn out, but now you've eaten and had a couple of drinks and are all clean, so you'll be discussing topic number one.''

Jim made the mistake of being polite and said, ''What?''

''Tail,'' she said.

At the far end of the room, glasses in hand, and looking as though they were having an unimportant *tête à tête*, were Moon and Franny. For the moment no one was within earshot.

Moon said, voice low, ''Why don't we get the hell out of here? Obviously, my cover is blown. And those Apaches must have a couple of hundred thousand gun-happy cloddies after them. That's all we need.''

Franny said, smiling brightly up into his face as though he had just made some off-the-cuff clever remark, ''I've been in contact with the National Executive Committee of the party. Everything's popping.''

His eyes went to hers quickly. ''How do you mean?'' He took an easy pull at his drink.

''We're surfacing. The Posterity Party is emerging from underground. We're going to start beating our drums as of tomorrow.''

''Too soon,'' he growled.

''Perhaps, but that's what the National Executive Committee has decided. The Second Constitutional Convention has become a farce. And this ridiculous foul-up with the Apaches has made the country look like an anachronistic . . .''

"Wait a minute," Moon said, nonchalantly sipping at his drink again, and laughing lightly as though they were telling jokes. "How about us? Our cover is blown. If this guy Shay knew how to find us, then so does whatever outfit he's working with."

She tried to keep anxiety from her voice. "The Executive Committee doesn't know about Shay. Your latest pamphlet is scheduled to hit the streets tomorrow. It's expected to be a bombshell. They want to be able to get hold of you at a moment's notice."

"Yeah," Moon said. "Fine. If that bastard doesn't get me first. Didn't you tell them . . .''

"I didn't know. When I came back, he was here. But, Ross, we can stick it out for a few hours. There's only one of him and three of us. And with these Indians around, cluttering up the situation . . .''

"Three of us?"

"I told you. You've forgotten. Max Cohn is our sole representative in Coronado. He's a party member."

"Oh, great. If he can tear his eyes away from that JoJo kid, he'll be a big help. It never occurred to me that I'd ever be anti-Semitic, but I've never seen a Jew in love before."

"Shut up," she said. "I'll try and get in contact with the N.E.C. later tonight. I think they've got something in mind for you tomorrow morning. Meanwhile, for Christ's sake, don't let yourself get caught alone with our pal, Jack."

"I'm going for another drink," Moon growled.

He got it and wandered over to where Bitter Joe and

Buffalo Dong were talking with several others standing around.

Bitter Joe said, "What the hell are you crazed Indians up to? You've got the whole country in an uproar."

"Shucks," Jim said from the sidelines, dragging his eyes away from Sweet Alice momentarily. "We've got the whole world in an uproar."

Buffalo Dong took a heavy slug of the applejack Doc had provided him with. "It's obvious, isn't it? We're trying to get back some of what was ripped off of us."

"But this burning down towns and blowing up bridges and all," Bitter Joe said. "Where will it end?"

"What burning down towns? What blowing up bridges?" Buffalo Dong said. "Does it look as if we four could . . ."

"Whatd'ya mean, four?" Zack said. "You mean all this stuff we've been hearing on the news was pulled off by your little outfit?"

"Yep, but most of it indirectly," Buffalo Dong admitted. "It's like that smart old biddy of yours said, we've got so many of the tribe in Mexico and France and the Reunited Nations and all, we four are the only ones left to be the army. There's only 268 remaining members of the tribe anyway, including old folks and kids."

All in on the discussion were gaping at him.

"The whites are doing all the trouble themselves," Jim said reasonably. "They're always dropping tear gas on each other, all that sort of crap. One time, their strategists decided they'd pin us down, so they destroyed a bunch of bridges, while we were actually a couple of hundred miles away. Then, when they found out they hadn't trapped us, they didn't have any bridges to get over the rivers. I tell you, they're as far around the bend as you can get."

"The military mind," Buffalo Dong said solemnly, swigging his drink again. He was beginning to show signs of the effect of Doc's potent product.

"What's a military mind?" Colleen said.

"The owner can take his shirt off without unbuttoning his collar," Buffalo Dong told her. "Have you ever read the accounts of most of the generals of this country? From Washington through Grant, who was loaded at Cold Harbor, through Custer, who didn't know the Indian's gun was loaded, through Eisenhower, who was playing golf a couple of hundred miles away when the important part of the Battle of the Bulge was being joined, to . . ."

"All right, all right," Bitter Joe said. "But what in the hell do you expect to get out of all this?"

"Some of what's coming to us," Marcy said indignantly. "We've been living on that flea-ridden reservation for over a century. We must be owed at least a million dollars per tribal member. Holy mackerel, we Apaches used to own more than half the state."

Franny got hold of Max Cohn and dragged him off to one side. Before she could say anything to him he said anxiously, "See here, you're a Chutzpa family member, is there any reason why I couldn't marry JoJo?"

She took him in. "How in the world would I know? Why don't you ask her?"

He was blank. "It didn't occur to me."

Franny said in disgust, "Wherefore art thou an idiot, Romeo? Now, listen, goddamn it, we're in the clutch. The chips are down, and everything's fucked-up to hell and gone."

He wrenched his mind away from the prospects of marrying JoJo. "How do you mean?"

"You didn't know Moon was Ross Prager, did you?"

"Who?"

"Ross Prager. Ross Prager. *Moon is Ross Prager*. The Party is keeping him undercover. I'm fronting for him. His new pamphlet is going to be issued simultaneously all over the country tomorrow. The shit is going to hit the fan. At the same time, the Posterity Party is going to reveal itself."

"The what is going to what?"

"Never mind. I shouldn't have put it that way, to a nice boy like you. The thing is, Ross has got to stay put here until we hear from the National Executive Committee about what he's to do. Maybe they need him for rallies or Tri-Di broadcasts, I don't know. The thing is, you and I are the only ones available to protect him meanwhile. And this guy Shay is probably a government gunman." She added sarcastically, "You've heard about the FBI and the CIA, I assume. You realize that it's possible for the government to have gunmen?"

"Now, wait a minute," he said in revolt. "Ross Prager is the reason I joined the Posterity Party—because of his pamphlets. You . . . you mean, that . . . that . . . I mean over there. That's Ross Prager?"

"Yeah," she said bitterly. "That's why I joined too."

"The one who makes the little dog talk?"

"As ever was."

"But he's a drunk. He's . . ."

"He's also a lousy lay. Right in the middle of tossing in bed with you, he'll get vague and then, out of a clear sky, get up and start making notes. I've been playing babysitter for this guy for the past three months. The one who had the job before me is doing twenty years on a trumped-up charge."

He stared at her and was doubly shocked to see that her eyes were moist. Franny was not the type to have tears in her eyes.

She said flatly, though almost weakly: "He's a genius, Max Cohn, and the hope of the Posterity Party."

"But . . . well, I thought he'd be, well, inspiring. Like, well, like Thomas Paine in the American revolution."

"Tom Paine was a bottle baby, Max—a drunk. For that matter, so were a lot of the others, the politico-economic thinkers. In the American labor movement, Eugene V. Debs, not to speak of other rebels such as Jack London. Or Bukharin, in Russia."

"Bukharin?"

"He was the man who did most of Lenin's thinking for him. The party theoretician of the Bolsheviks. Stalin finally had him shot. He was dangerous; he could think. When Stalin took over, he didn't want any thinkers around, not even rummies."

Max Cohn groaned. "What do we do?"

"We can't let Moon out of our sight. I get the feeling that Shay is under orders to handle this with kid gloves. It can't be obvious. Hopefully, as long as Moon is in a room with other people, Shay won't make his play. So we'll both stick as near to him as possible."

Moon had rejoined the group around Bitter Joe and Buffalo Dong.

The family iconoclast was saying, "But, Sarge, how the hell can you expect a couple of hundred of you Indians to defeat the whole United States of the Americas? Especially when you can only put four of you into the field, including one girl."

"We've got things working for us," Buffalo Dong said, his voice slightly blurry from the applejack. "Mostly, their stupidity. They haven't had any troubles with Indians for over a century, except that thing up at Wounded Knee. They don't know how to handle it. They're on the hysterical side. Yesterday, another tanker sank off the coast of Alaska. The second since we declared war. Immediately, the damn fools allowed the media to shout sabotage, blaming it on us. And you know what that led to? Lloyds of London has declared American shipping insurance upped to wartime emergency levels.''

Zack said blankly, ''Well, what of it?'' He had his new leather baton in his hands and had been absently slapping it into his left palm as he listened in.

''What of it?'' the Indian chief chortled. ''It means that American shipping will be paying hundreds of millions of pseudo-dollars more for insurance than any other country. They won't be able to compete on the world market. A howl will go up for peace at any price from all corporations involved in shipping.''

Ron said, wide-eyed, ''Did you really sink those ships?''

''Hell, no,'' Hank said in disgust. ''How could the four of us sabotage a tanker off Alaska? It's like Eskiminzin said. They're hysterical. Can you imagine how much money they've spent already sending two Army Corps down into this country?''

''And all the heat being stirred up in Europe and all,'' Jim said. ''Cripes, every country in the world with a grudge against Uncle Sam is jumping in, yelling blue murder. Colonialism, imperialism! What a laugh.''

Moon said, really interested, ''Do you think the government'll capitulate?''

''Well, we're banking on it,'' Buffalo Dong said. ''It's the easy way out for them. If we can just stick to our guns for a little while longer.''

Moon took another pull at his current drink. ''The whole handling of the Indians was ridiculous from the beginning,'' he growled. ''Typical lack of planning. There were a lot of

jobs the Indians could have fitted into, where they would
have been priceless. Forest rangers, for instance; fire war-
dens up in timber country, sheep herders, cowboys—the
plains Indians were born horsemen. Or prospectors. Nobody could possibly know the mountains and deserts in
this part of the country like the Apaches. But no, instead
of utilizing the best materials at hand, we recruited our
westerners from the slums of the East. People like Billy
the Kid, Wyatt Earp, Wild Bill Hickok. Gunmen, scum,
misfits and malcontents, fugitives from justice and just plain
bums. They're the ones who took over the West. They
died like flies doing it—and it couldn't have happened to
nicer people.''

Buffalo Dong looked over at him, calculatingly. ''Who
the devil are you?''

''Name's Prager. Ross Prager,'' the other said, taking
still another slug of his drink.

Marcy looked at him, her eyes narrowed. ''You're
kidding. No, I guess you're not. I'll be damned. I've read
a couple of your pamphlets. Life is only—uh, I forget,''
she trailed off.

Bitter Joe and Buffalo Dong looked at her in sorrow.

She said apologetically, ''You know me; always in there
punchy.''

The two old-timers started off on another tangent, and
Franny sidled up to Moon. She said, in a whisper, ''Where
the devil is Shay?''

He looked at her, his eyes slightly bleary. ''How would
I know?''

She said, ''He's not around. I don't like it.''

John Shay was out of the underground dwelling and
about two hundred yards off to one side on the grass,

where he could see in all directions. He had his wrist tight-beam communicator to his mouth.

"Shay here, Shay here," he said urgently.

A voice faded in. "Receiving you. Hold for a few minutes, please."

"Holding." Shay said, a faint snarl in the background of his voice.

In less than five minutes, the Director's voice faded in, faint and tinny, as usual. "Very well, Thomas here."

"I'm talking fast, before I might be interrupted. I'm on the Chutzpa place. I don't think I've been made except by the de Rudder broad. Prager's here."

"Any way of getting to him . . . accidentally? Things are beginning to pop with his organization. We're not sure, but something's in the wind. We want him finished."

"All right, all right. You want him to be hit accidentally, right?"

"That was your instruction," the Director said impatiently.

"That's right. There's some bombers not too far off, aren't there?"

"Bombers!"

"Yeah, that's right. Bombers, bombers. Out after the Indians."

"What's that got to do with hitting Ross Prager accidentally?"

"Have them come over and blast this Chutzpa place off the map. You must have the coordinates in the National Data Banks. The whole place is in a small valley. And there's nobody else living in it for miles around."

"What . . . what . . . ? Have you gone completely drivel-happy?"

"No. Buffalo Dong and his gang are here. They've

been received like relatives. Okay. Send the bombers over. Knock the place off the map. You'll get the goddamned Indians and at the same time Prager and his bimbo, Francesca de Rudder. And when all the smoke clears up, it'll all look like an accident, the fact that he was here when the Air Force got the Indians. Either that, or it'll look like he was in with them, which is just as good.''

"But . . . but, how about you?''

"Send them over in two hours. I'll be long gone.''

"Now wait a minute. Those damned Apaches are armed with Russian laser rifles. They could knock our planes out of the skies, especially since they'd have to come in low in the mountain country there.''

John Shay said, "They don't have laser assault rifles. They're fakes. I got a close look at one of them. They're models of the real guns. Buffalo Dong and his men must have copied them out of some magazines or one of those gun books; the only functional parts are the laser sights, which you can buy at any good gun shop. In short, Thomas, they're unarmed. Send the bombers over in two hours, and wipe out everything living within a four-mile radius. They won't be able to get out of that.''

Director Roy Thomas was a man of decision. He said, "You've got it, Shay. Two hours,'' and flicked off the phone.

Chapter Twenty

John Shay didn't return to the main dwelling of the Chutzpa family but, instead, made his way to the Kid Kolony and to the room he had taken over from Sweet Alice.

He packed his bag, not particularly hurrying. When the chips were all down, John Shay was a man of icy calm.

A voice from the doorway said, "Going somewhere?"

Shay looked up, tensing only slightly. His gun was ready at hand, in his belt. It was one of the younger Indians, the one they called Hank.

Shay said, "Yeah."

The other shook his head. "I don't think that'd be a very good idea. Not as long as we're here. It's not that we don't trust you, or that you're a prisoner, or anything. But we just can't afford to take chances."

The professional assassin's lips hardly moved. He said, "What're you going to do about it?"

Hank frowned, displeased about the whole situation. He wasn't sure just where this one fitted in. He didn't seem to be a regular member of the Chutzpa family. Nor did that other one, Max Cohn, the lovelorn cube. The family, of course, had already proven themselves A-1 in the eyes of the four Apaches. On top of which, evidently Eskiminzin and the old boy they called Bitter Joe had served together in the Asian War. No, the family were not to be faulted, but where did this one fit in?

Hank said, "Tell you what: let's go back to the main house and talk it over with the rest."

It was Shay's turn to think about it. His best bet was to clear out without trouble. If he started something, it might develop in some unforeseen direction. He had no time for hassles, and he came to a quick decision.

"All right," he said. "Let's go. The family will vouch for me. I was just dropping by on my way through. I'd like to get going."

He picked up his bag in his left hand, leaving his right free to draw the .38 Noiseless tucked in his belt beneath his jacket, and led the way. Hank followed, not overly upset about this development, but wanting to see it through.

They entered the saloon through the patio, and Shay put his bag down near the door before advancing further into the room. All the family members were present, save the twins. And all looked up, first at the two, and then all eyes went to the suitcase.

"Going somewhere, Jack?" Blackie said, her graying eyebrows up. She was in her old-fashioned rocking chair, knitting.

Shay managed one of his tight smiles. "That's right," he said. "I thought I'd split. It's nice here and a pleasure to meet you all, but I've got business on the coast."

Buffalo Dong scowled; looked first at Bitter Joe and then at Blackie, an apologetic expression on his swarthy face. He said, "I was hoping that we four could stay here until morning. We could use the rest."

And the Professor said, "Yes, of course. Why not?"

Buffalo Dong said, the apology in his voice now, "I don't think it's practical for us to stay, if someone has left. Anything might happen and it might come out that we're around."

Shay said, in injured voice, "You think I'd inform on you?"

Rusty said, "This is a helluva time to leave, Jack. You don't figure on driving all night, do you? Why not stay on until morning? Get a fresh start. And then our Apache friends, here, won't have to worry."

"I just have the urge to go now."

Bitter Joe said to the Indian chief, "You can trust Jack. He's the boyfriend of a former family member."

"Bullshit," Blackie said, in her usual placid voice. "He never met Nora in his life."

Suddenly the expressions on the faces of all the older family members indicated that they realized the truth of that. More or less subconsciously, the fact had been suspected; but now they all knew it to be true.

All eyes went to Shay, who stood near the door.

"I don't want to argue," he said, as though weary. "I'm going. So long." He turned and began to bend to pick up the bag.

Franny shot a look at Moon, who was also scowling puzzlement at this development.

Jim said easily, "I'm afraid you're going to have to stay until morning anyway, Jack."

The other straightened and turned, his right hand only

inches from the edge of his jacket. "Oh? Why?" he said, his tone dangerous.

"You've got three cars here. Franny's in the garage, two parked out front, yours and Max's. Before we came in and found out you were friends, I jimmied all three of them. I doubt like hell that we could repair any tonight—even if we wanted to."

John Shay's face went empty. "I'm getting out of here anyway," he said tightly. "I'll walk into Coronado and rent a car, or take a bus."

"Why?" Franny said to him. "It doesn't make sense. It's a dark, moonless night. What in the world's your hurry?"

"None of your goddamned business." He began to turn again.

Moon said conversationally to Bitter Joe and Buffalo Dong, "Shay came here after me. He's probably working for the Division of Clandestine Services, though I've got no proof of that."

Marcy said, "Holy Mackerel," and then, "If you can't trust him, neither can we!"

And suddenly there was a short-barreled pistol in the right hand of John Shay, comfortably, competently held. The saloon's occupants froze.

"See here," Max Cohn blurted without meaning, from where he sat on a couch next to JoJo.

Shay half turned again, moving in a sidestep in the direction of his bag. Bowser was in the way, sitting there, the tip of his tongue out, and taking in this drama between the humans. Shay snarled, "Get out of the way, Mutt," kicked the little dog aside, and began to stoop for the suitcase, still keeping his eyes carefully on the occupants of the room.

He would have done better to watch the diminutive mongrel. Bowser had had enough from this source. He came in for the kill, and sank his small teeth into the enemy's lower calf.

Ruthie was near and among the least noticed of those present. She stepped in quickly and kicked him, as hard as her nine years allowed, in the shin. "I told you you'd be sorry you weren't nice to me," she shrilled, proving again the adage that hell hath no fury like a nymphet scorned.

The gunman shook off the hairy little animal and booted him to the far end of the room.

But that was time enough.

Zack jerked his leather baton from his hip pocket and pressed something on its side. A leather thong shot out from its end, reaching out several yards in Shay's direction. As if by magic, the end of it wrapped around the gun. Zack jerked, and the gun fell to the floor.

The four Indians, the Chutzpa family and Moon were all frozen, overwhelmed by the rapid developments.

John Shay snarled, swooped quickly to scoop up the gun again.

It was then that Max Cohn entered the fray. He leapt up from the couch, shouting, *"Kaiii!"* his arms flailing like windmills, his hands chopping the air, his feet seemingly kicking out in half a dozen directions at once.

Shay's eyes had barely the time to widen before Max was on him in a flurry of vicious blows, kicks, and even a butt of the head. The last of the hit men collapsed to the floor.

Rusty said, "Christ."

Jim and Hank were on the fallen one immediately. Ron darted in and snatched up the gun and backed quickly away.

Zack touched the side of his leather handle again and the thong shot back into it. He was beaming pleasure. "Golly," he crowed. "I told you I'd come up with a gimmick novelty. It'll sweep the country. An automated miniature bullwhip."

Blackie said complacently, "Tie the bastard up, boys."

Doc left, to return from the kitchen in moments with a roll of heavy twine.

"Let me do that," Buffalo Dong growled, taking the cord from the other. "It's been a long time, but in my day I've tied up so many gooks I could do it in my sleep."

They stretched the still-unconscious John Shay out on one of the couches. And then, without a word, filed over to the bar for drinks.

JoJo, her eyes shining adoration, said to Max, "Darling, what in the world did you do?"

Franny was also staring at him, almost in accusation. "You took the words right out of my mouth, JoJo," she said.

Max was embarrassed. His adam's apple bobbed twice and then he said to Franny, "When I joined up with the Posterity Party, I thought I ought to learn how to handle myself in an emergency. So I took a course on the Tri-Di Auto-Teacher in Kenpo."

Franny said blankly, "On the Tri-Di Auto-Teacher? Who did you practice with?"

"Nobody," he said, an element of apology in his voice. "Just by myself."

"Jesus," Bowser said. He had recovered from the flurry of action a few minutes before and was now sitting near the couch that held the unconscious man, eyeing Shay in obvious satisfaction.

Rusty was looking down at Shay, a glass of applejack in

her hand. "I don't like it," she said. "Why was he in such a fit to get away?"

Franny, also equipped with a glass, looked about at the others, her eyes narrowing. "How many phones do you have in this house? Any more than we had when I was here last?"

Bitter Joe caught her drift and shook his head. "Only the one on the desk over there."

Franny said, "Has anybody seen this louse using it any time today, and especially tonight?"

Nobody had and someone had always been in the room whenever Shay had been present.

"So he couldn't have communicated with anybody on the outside," Rusty said. "But I still don't like it. Somebody throw a bucket of water on the sonofabitch."

Colleen went into the kitchen for the water.

Ron handed Shay's altered gun to Buffalo Dong, saying, "Here, you better take this. I don't know anything about guns."

The Indian took it, but shrugged and said, "It's been over twenty years since I handled one myself."

Zack looked at the three laser rifles that leaned against the wall. "How do you mean?"

"They're not guns," the Indian told him sourly. "They're mock-ups; props with low-power laser sights. We didn't want to hurt anybody. And, obviously, even if we did, we couldn't fight the whole U.S. Army."

"Holy smokes," Moon said in awe. "What a war. Two Army Corps and God only knows how many squadrons of aircraft on one side, all gung-ho for slaughter, and on the other, three unarmed men and a nurse."

Colleen returned with a plastic bucket full of water and

poured it with satisfaction over the soon-sputtering John Shay.

He shook his head, yanked without any success at all his bonds, and then stared up at them, his eyes wide. All were gathered around returning the stare, save Blackie who had never budged from her chair and her knitting through all that had transpired.

Shay got out in a rush, "How long have I been under?"

Moon looked down at him and improvised. "Oh, long enough," he said carefully.

"I got to get out of here," Shay rasped.

Rusty said, "Great. Why?"

Shay clammed up for the moment, but his eyes were shifting, almost darting. He was obviously trying to figure it through, trying to come up with angles. He shook his head.

"Listen," he said. "Loosen me. I gotta call it off."

"Call what off?" Franny demanded.

"The air strike, dammit!"

Silence fell.

Chapter Twenty-One

"What air strike?" Moon said finally.

It came out in a rush. "I reported that you and the Indians were all here. They're sending in bombers to flatten this whole area for about four miles around. There won't be so much as a guinea hen left alive by time they're through. Let me get at my communicator. On my wrist. I'll call it all off."

"Who're you working for?" Franny said.

He hesitated, then blurted, "For Roy Thomas. He hired me to finish Ross Prager."

Moon—Ross Prager—grunted scorn. "Hired you?" he said. "You mean, you don't even belong to his Division?"

"No. I'm a . . . free lancer. He wanted to keep it ultra-secret."

Ross Prager's laugh was a deprecation. "And you think that he'd let you call it off, Shay? Don't be stupid. This way, he'll *really* keep it secret. Not even you will be able to talk. And all of us will be so much churned up hamburger that they'll probably never even identify the bodies. Think of something else, Shay. And you'd better think fast. How much time do we have?''

"Two hours," Shay said hurriedly, "from when I phoned Thomas. Maybe less. Untie me! We'll have to make a run for it.''

Bitter Joe said, "Run four miles, on a pitch-black night, most of the way without a road, in an hour and a half? This is rugged country once you're off our cultivated area, Shay. It'd take us an hour to stagger a mile, even if nobody managed to break a leg along the way. And we'd have to carry the twins and maybe Ruthie, when she tuckered out.''

Shay said, terror behind his pale eyes now, "We gotta get out of here.''

Blackie said, knitting away, "This prick doesn't have any ideas. Does anybody else? We're about to be converted into a family fondue.''

Franny, breathing in pants, snapped, "JoJo, Sweet Alice: run quick. Get me any make-up you have on hand. A couple of hairbrushes. Your best face mirror. Quick, goddamn it!''

The girls scooted without asking questions.

Now all stares were directed to the rocket-set girl.

"Franny, have you slipped your cogs?" Rusty said.

"No," Franny rapped. She turned her attention to Colleen and Rusty and snapped, "Get me the most attractive scarf you've got in the place. Quick! I don't have a damn thing in my luggage. Something bright.''

She spun to Buffalo Dong, who stood slightly to one side, flanked by his three Apaches.

She snapped, "Will you settle for one million pseudo-dollars for every man, woman and child in the Marijuanero Apache tribe?''

''Ugh,'' Buffalo Dong said, for once meaning it. ''What?''

''You heard me. A million psuedo-dollars for every tribal member, in return for calling the war off.''

His Indian stoicism was gone with the snows of yesteryear. ''I . . . uh, it's not up to me. *A million for every tribal member!* That's a quarter of a billion pseudo-dollars!''

''Like shit it's not up to you! You're the War Chief. And you four are the only Marijuanero Apaches left in New Mexico. Put it to a goddam vote, if you want to. And get into your war paint.''

She hurried over to the saloon's desk and plopped down into the chair before the phone screen, even as JoJo and Sweet Alice came dashing back into the room, laden down with hand mirrors, hairbrushes and their small supply of cosmetics. The Chutzpa girls had never relied much on make-up.

Franny groaned at the meagre supply. ''For Christ's sake,'' she said. ''Don't you have any eye shade? Quick, JoJo, start combing my hair.''

As the brunette complied, Franny grabbed up a hand mirror and began working on her face with the cosmetics. In moments she was a different Franny. When Colleen entered the room with a bright scarf, she grabbed it and tied it artfully about her neck.

She turned to the TV-phone screen and adjusted it so that her clothing couldn't be seen below the neckline.

She snapped to Buffalo Dong, Hank and Jim, who had, as ordered, replaced their war paint, ''Okay, you damned redskins, stand behind me, when I gesture for you. Have your phony guns in your hands. Damn it, I hope I can remember this number."

She took a deep breath, flicked on the phone screen and dialed.

A vapid face faded onto the screen, took Franny in, and eyes widened. The voice was high, artificial, brittle.

"Why, Francesca, dear. Where on Earth have you been? Nobody's seen you for months. I mean *months*, dahling. What is the rocket-set without our mad-cap Francesca?" Her eyes narrowed. "Are scarfs in again, dahling?"

Franny sighed. "Anything I wear becomes 'in,' Annabelle, as you very well know." She ran a languid hand back over her newly neatened hair, as though exhausted. "Oh, Annabelle, dahling, I'm afraid that this little scoop is too late for your regular society gossip broadcast, but don't you have some way of breaking in for flash announcements?"

The other's face changed slightly, a bit worriedly. She said with caution, "Well, yes, dahling. But it has to be something really big, you know. I'm afraid if it's just a matter of your announcing an engagement . . . unless it was to somebody really *big*, you know, dahling . . ." Annabelle looked even vaguer than before, and let her words dribble away.

Franny sighed wearily again. "Oh, nothing so mundane as that, dear. You see, my life is in immediate danger."

The society gossip newscaster gaped at her. 'Now *really*, Francesca dahling, aren't you being a trifle melodramatic? What could possibly happen to Francesca de Rudder?"

"I'm quite serious, dear Annabelle. "I've joined the Posterity Party. Not for just a lark, you know. I'm quite serious, dahling. And it seems that Roy Thomas . . ."

"Oh, that re*pul*sive man! He was at a cocktail party the other evening and . . ."

Francesca went on, ". . . is sending over bombers to destroy me and Chief Buffalo Dong and that dahling political writer, Ross Prager. We're all here on a small farm in New Mexico. And Ross Prager, on his own initiative, has come to terms with the Apaches. Such a ridiculously handled affair from the beginning. But now everything is settled."

The woman on the phone screen was still gawking. "Buffalo Dong . . ." she said weakly.

The three stalwart Apaches responded to Franny's gesture and lined up behind her, so that they could be seen in the screen, complete with guns and warpaint.

Annabelle gasped.

Franny said, "This is Buffalo Dong and two of his sub-chiefs, dahling. Chief, this is Annabelle, the most influential feminine commentator on Tri-Di."

Buffalo Dong took his cue and said, "Ugh."

Annabelle said desperately, "But . . . but . . . come to terms? Dahling, whatever do you mean?"

"Oh, Ross Prager is ever so clever. He's solved it all. He's made them agree to sign a treaty, turning over their whole reservation, with all its uranium, to the government for only a quarter of a billion pseudo-dollars. Heavens, dahling, the Army and Air Force are spending that much a week blowing up bridges and shooting each other."

Annabelle was still gawking. "But Francesca, what if the government doesn't back Mr. Prager?"

Franny fluffed her hair in irritation; tossed her head. "In that case, which is unlikely, I personally pledge to meet the whole amount, if it takes every pseudo-dollar in my portfolio." She cleared her throat and added definitely,

"Including those in numbered accounts in Switzerland, the Bahamas, Hong Kong and Costa Rica. Oh, dear, I do hope I shan't have to give up my Costa Rican bonds. They're so cute, all gold-embossed and all. But really, dahling, you must hurry and put pressure to bear, don't you know, dear? The bombers are probably already on the way."

"Dahling, I'll be on a world-wide network within ten minutes. And when that's through, I'll call Martha in the New White House, direct. Our First Lady will be simply *fur*ious. Martha adores you, of course."

The face faded and Franny collapsed back into her chair.

Moon looked at her. All the rest of the family had collapsed as well onto couches or chairs. Save for Ruthie who had ignored the boring adult phone call and was eyeing Zack, accusingly.

Moon said, "It's out of our hands, now. Do you really have that much money?"

"No," Franny told him. "But everybody thinks I do. And I don't have any numbered accounts, either. But again, everybody thinks I do."

Moon contemplated her as she slumped there, trembling with tension. "That was done with verve," he said. "Will you marry me?"

"Ha," she said. "All of you male chauvinist pigs, to use the old term, want to marry me for my wealth."

"Yeah, well—true," he admitted. "But you're also a great lay."

Ruthie was still staring at Zack, a thumb in her mouth. "Zack," she said accusingly, "What's a bullwhip? And how'd you do that there?"

He beamed at her. Nobody else, in spite of his feat, had gotten around to him as yet. He brought his baton gadget from his hip pocket. "The bullwhip was too big. Winding it around your waist was too much trouble. So I worked up this deal where the whip part is in the handle and you push this little stud and it flicks out, real fast. And you can do your tricks like Zorro and the gauchos down on the Argentine pampas. Understand?"

"Not a word of it," Ruthie said. "What's a bullwhip?"

Franny was eyeing the bound John Shay. "You know," she said, "we ought to get a statement from this character. All about Roy Thomas assigning him to finish off Ross. It can be presented at the Second Constitutional Convention when the Posterity Party surfaces tomorrow."

"I'm not talking," Shay said in contempt.

Bitter Joe said, "Hell, turn him over to Buffalo Dong. He was going to have them bombed, too. The Apaches know all about that sort of thing."

Buffalo Dong said, "Ugh. That squaw work. Turn paleface over to our squaw. Her grandmother, Low-Slung Fanny, best in tribe at that sort of thing."

"Ugh." Marcy said, going over to her nurse's kit. She opened it and began to bring forth scalpels, surgical scissors, and other impressive instruments.

"On the other hand," Shay said quickly, "I'm talking. I'm talking, I'm talking . . ."

Blackie said, over her knitting, "I wonder if they'll stop the fucking bombers in time. Don't you think we ought to have a few quick ones while Moon gets Jack's confession? If we *do* get bombed I'd rather be bombed to start with."

They all looked at her with respect.

And Bowser said, "Life is but a limber dick in the cruddy jockstrap of time."

Marcy, laughing, looked down at him. "You know, I'm

beginning to like you," she said. "In spite of your moth-eaten appearance."

He put his tongue out a half-inch, panted and said, "You're not so bad yourself, puppy."

From the corner of the room came Franny's command as Annabelle's face assembled itself on the Tri-Di screen: "All right, you booze-freaks: drink a toast to Annabelle, here, and pray that she pulls this off!"

Aftermath

Max Cohn looked over at the gorgeous brunette on the pillow next to him. Her smile was dazzling.

His adam's apple bobbed and he said, "Uh, darling, will you marry me?"

Her eyes rounded. "Well, good heavens, why, dear?"

He looked at her emptily. "Well, you know. We'll have a family, children and all."

"But I have a family. I'm a Chutzpa. *I love my family. I like to live here. If you want, you can come and I'm sure everybody would vote you in as a member of the family."*

"And everybody would raise the children?" he said in despair. "Even Zack and Sweet Alice?"

"Well, yes, of course. And Blackie, and Bitter Joe and the Professor and . . . everybody."

He closed his eyes and inwardly groaned. What would his mother have said had she learned he changed his name to Chutzpa?

Walter Hammond, Chief Engineer of the Department Of Mining, looked up slowly and let his eyes run about the horizon. As far as he could see, there was the near waste-land of Geronimo County, former reservation of the Marijuanero Apaches.

His assistant, inferring that something was wrong, said, "What's the matter, sir?"

Hammond said slowly, "I should have remembered that three of those damned redskins took their mining engineer's degrees at MIT."

"I beg your pardon, sir?"

Hammond looked up at him wearily. "These supposed uranium deposits? Salted. Uncle Sam has paid out a quarter of a billion pseudo-dollars for possibly the most worthless chunk of real estate in North America."

The expression on his assistant's face was blank. He said, "I saw on a newscast the other day that the whole tribe has taken off for Switzerland. They've all bought chalets on the shores of Lake Geneva."

THE LIVING END